ON ICE:
POWER PLAY BOOK 2

L. Anne Carrington

Palm Tree Books

"There will always be people who doubt me and want to see me fail and every time I step on the ice, it is my job to prove people wrong."

— Sidney Crosby, Pittsburgh Penguins captain

Power Play Series by L. Anne Carrington

Power Play
On Ice: Power Play Book 2
The O'Freels : Power Play Book 3 (coming 2017)

The Post-*Power Play* Years

The fishing port of Yarmouth, Nova Scotia perches defiantly on the tip of the middle finger Nova Scotia, extending to the battering waves of the North Atlantic.

Troy Talmadge and his short-statured wife Alex spent each summer in a custom-built four-bedroom residence overlooking the sea. Their home featured high ceilings vaulting to the second floor, a winding staircase, expansive windows, Olympic-sized pool, and gargantuan basement recreation area that include a fitness room and indoor hockey rink.

The Talmadge's wedding portrait hangs beside an oil painting of two girls and a boy dressed in hockey jerseys hung side by side above the fireplace mantel.

Anastazie "Anna" Ivanka, Alex's daughter by a previous marriage, wore her father's now-retired Miami Sun Devils number 84, and Alex's two children with Troy in Pittsburgh Rebels jerseys; son Quinn's emblazoned with Troy's 77 and daughter Noémie donned Alex's 33.

Quinn and Noémie Talmadge attended St. Robinson–Twin Lakes Academy in Pittsburgh during the school year, and from where Anna Ivanka graduated with honors . "St. Rob's" is a co-ed private school, an ultimate choice for the offspring of executives, financiers, medical professionals, attorneys, athletes, and celebrities. In addition to its strong academic curriculum, St. Rob's is known for its solid literary, theater, hockey, basketball, football, soccer, and tennis programs.

Czech-American stunner Anna stood five feet, eight inches with a full-breasted, flawless figure most teenage girls yearned to emulate, crystalline blue eyes, and mocha-colored curls tumbled over her shoulders. Her ebullient personality drew people from all walks of life, making her one of St. Rob's most popular girls. She played left wing for the girls' hockey team, an honor student, cheerleader, homecoming queen, debate team standout, former Miss Pennsylvania Teen Princess, and runner up to Miss American Teen Princess.

Anna traveled each summer with her Czechoslovakian father, AHC Hall of Fame member Jakuas "Jax" Ivanka, training for her own career in professional hockey and assisting with his various business ventures. She eventually relocated to the Czech Republic after being drafted in the fifth round by the Prague Capitals.

Anna's mother and stepfather dealt with headaches that accompanied refereeing her squabbles with younger half-brother Quinn Talmadge while both lived at home.

The little girl who sneaked into baby Quinn's nursery to sleep near his crib, comforted him when he cried, and rarely let him out of her sight grew annoyed with his presence during their teen years before once again developing a close bond between occasional lighthearted bantering.

Noémie Talmadge had her mother's short stature and physical features. Family members nicknamed her "Pickle;" Troy would often jokingly state – much to Alex's displeasure – that Noémie looked like a life-sized gherkin at birth.

A bright, compassionate child perhaps pampered by her parents and siblings, Noémie earned respectable grades at St. Rob's elementary school though she struggled in math. She loved reading and creative writing; teachers entered several of her short stories in literary contests, many winning awards.

Noémie viewed herself shadowed by her famous parents and accomplished siblings, but shone in her own right as a champion jumper in horse shows. The elfin girl and her horse, Blazing Fire, were mainstays on the circuit, winning blue ribbon after blue ribbon.

She also rode for other prestigious owners when not studying English-style riding, equestrienne, and jumping with some of the United States' and Canada's most elite trainers.

She gave her parents little trouble and remained close to Quinn and Anna, but Noémie barely concealed her feelings of envy when Troy interacted with other children at public appearances.

He was *her* daddy; she always disliked sharing him with anyone except family members and friends.

Troy reminded his youngest child that meeting other kids were part of his and Alex's jobs, some not as lucky to have loving parents, living in nice houses with plenty of food, proper clothing, and receiving quality educations as Noémie and her siblings were.

The Talmadge household wasn't always a perfect one, but Anna, Quinn, and Noémie were blessed having Alex and Troy lending them strong support through learning life's many lessons; some difficult, others pleasant.

Occasional sibling rivalries aside, each sibling stood behind the others throughout roads traveled to reach their respective milestones – with Quinn Talmadge's perhaps being both the most arduous and brightest.

***

PART ONE

Quinn

"Sometimes it just feels like the only thing you do is play hockey and eat."

- Henrik Lundqvist

Chapter 1

Quinn Parker Talmadge was born a precious gift to his parents. While Troy enjoyed his role as Anna's doting stepfather, he and Alex yearned for a family of their own. They welcomed their first child together two weeks after Anna's third birthday, albeit with an unsettling beginning.

Alex fell ill while she and Troy visited his family in Nova Scotia. She was only 30 weeks into gestation when paramedics rushed her to Yarmouth Regional Hospital with toxemia and high blood pressure, no one sure if she or the baby would survive.

Doctors delivered Quinn via emergency C-section and he barely weighed three pounds at birth. Alex never saw such a tiny infant; he appeared fragile and too small to handle.

A delivery room nurse informed Troy and his family that Quinn had little chance of survival. They refused to believe the news; Troy insisted everything possible be done to save his son, no matter what cost or length of time it took.

The baby pulled through, beating incredible odds. Quinn weighed five pounds after spending little over three weeks in an incubator, and his parents could finally take him home. Quinn brought joy to them and Anna immediately adored her new half-brother.

Following his rocky beginning – including a bout with colic – Quinn Talmadge thrived. He transitioned from a fragile baby into an adorable toddler, resembling Troy with one exception: he had Alex's distinctive violet eyes, complete with long, perfectly fanned lashes.

Both children were quick to turn over, sit, crawl, and talk, but Quinn still made no attempt to walk at eighteen months. Alex's in-laws and friends assured her each child matured at their own rate, and Quinn being a boy may have weighed in on the delay.

Alex took him to the pediatrician and insisted on a full battery of tests, convinced something was wrong with her son's legs.

"Quinn's tests revealed nothing abnormal," the doctor informed her. "He's doing well for a child born premature."

"He hasn't made any attempts to walk. Are you sure his legs are all right? My daughter- "

8

"Some children clear hurdles without difficulty while others struggle and bounce back most of the time. Quinn will walk when *he's* ready. Life isn't a race, Mrs. Talmadge; it's not supposed to be a race. You'll be surprised what your son achieves if you don't rush him. My only suggestion is to take Quinn home and let him progress at his own pace."

***

Quinn took his first steps three days after the pediatrician visit.

Anna rushed into the den where Alex attended to business on her laptop. "Mommy! Mommy!"

"What is it, honey? I'm in the middle of working."

"Baby! Come quick!"

"Where's Judy?"

"She's with him. Hurry, Mommy!"

Alex bolted from her chair. *Oh God, what's wrong?*

Fear turned to elation when she spotted Quinn standing upright staring at his feet, attempting to walk.

"Anna, why didn't you tell me?"

"Sorry, Mrs. Talmadge," the nanny said. "I told her not to say anything. We wanted to surprise you."

Alex handed Judy her phone. "Make sure you get video for Troy to watch when he comes home."

"Yes ma'am."

Quinn looked at Alex as if he'd done something wrong. "Mama?"

"Come here, honey; it's okay." She extended her arms and smiled. "Come see me."

Quinn took a few rudimentary steps.

"Look at my good boy! Keep coming to Mama."

Her encouragement increased Quinn's confidence and he continued waddling toward her and Judy.

"See, Mommy?" Anna said excitedly as Alex gathered him in her arms. "He walked!"

"Yes he did." Alex cuddled Quinn. "Our big boy!"

Judy returned Alex's phone. "I caught every minute on your phone, Mrs. Talmadge."

"Thanks. Looks like someone inherited Daddy's bowlegged waddle-walk. I can't wait to see Troy's reaction."

"He'll be thrilled." Judy rose from the floor. "I'll get the kids cleaned up for dinner."

***

Troy stared at Alex's phone when she placed it on the table. "Is this thing still giving you problems?"

"No, it's working fine. Judy helped me make something you should see."

He beamed with pride while watching the video. "I didn't know our nanny's a budding filmmaker."

"My idea; I wanted you to see our son's first steps."

"Why does exciting stuff happen when I'm not home?"

"Wait a minute, mister; you *were* here when Quinn started talking. As matter of fact, he spends more time with me, Judy, and Anna than anyone else, yet 'Daddy' and 'hockey' were among his first words."

Troy grinned and handed Alex the phone. "I guess my next step is buying the little man a pair of skates."

"Troy, he's barely walking."

"Dad put me on the ice when I was two."

"Aren't you rushing things? What if Quinn wants to someday pursue another career path?"

"Long as it isn't a bank robber, pimp, mass murderer or drug dealer, I'll support his decision."

"Even if you'd prefer he follow in our footsteps?"

"Why not? He and Anna enjoy going to Rebels games. Jax started training her last summer."

"You're not having any contests with my ex-husband, friendly or otherwise. I dealt with the two of you more than enough when we were all teammates."

"Who said anything about contests?"

Alex glared at him. "You know what I mean."

"At least let me teach Quinn to skate after he's walking a little longer. He may like it."

"All right, but don't act huffy if he doesn't."

"Promise!"

"Good. Go wash your hands; Judy's cleaning up the kids and Francine has dinner almost ready."

***

Chapter 2

Troy gently guided his 22-month-old son across the ice using a learner's support bar. "Come on, buddy; let Daddy show you how to skate."

"Hockey?" Quinn gave him a hopeful look.

"Let's learn to skate first."

"Noooo..."

"You're okay, little man. I won't leave you." Troy picked him up. "Let me show you skating can be fun before you try again."

"Hockey?"

"Not yet. We'll skate some more." Troy glided around the rink several times with Quinn in his arms. "See? Nothing scary."

Quinn pointed to his own feet. "My skates."

"Yes, and soon you'll be good as Daddy."

"Okay."

"Do you want to go again with the learner's support?"

Quinn wriggled in Troy's grasp. "Yeah!"

Troy placed him on the ice and readjusted him on the device used for helping young children learn to skate. "You're not scared anymore?"

"Uh uh."

"All right, here we go."

Troy paced a laughing Quinn under the rink's bright light, the icy air delectable as it filled their lungs. Troy often got cold on the ice during his early years playing hockey, but as decades passed, the cooled rink temperature suited him well, as if his body was built for chilly atmospheres.

He grimaced when an acrid odor suddenly invaded his nostrils. "Did you let a tooter, buddy?"

"Uh uh. Poopie."

"Oh, God; why didn't you tell me you needed to potty?" He scooped up Quinn and headed to the dressing area. "Good thing Judy packed extra things for you."

Troy changed his son's soiled diaper, trying not to gag from its offensive aroma as Quinn giggled.

"Laugh it up now, kid; it won't be funny when you're doing the same thing for me and Mommy someday."

"I poopie."

"You sure did, buddy. What do Mommy and Judy feed you? Phew! Stinky boy."

"Skate more?"

"After I finish cleaning you. Remind me when we get home to tell Mommy you need additional potty training before we proceed with any more hockey lessons."

***

Alex greeted Troy and Quinn with a welcoming smile. "My favorite men are home!"

Quinn held out his arms as Troy handed him to her. "Mama, I skate!"

She kissed his dark hair. "Good boy!"

Troy beamed. "Our little guy did well aside from being scared at first and filling his pants."

"I noticed. Your patience was endearing."

He looked befuddled. "Wait...what are you talking about?"

"Let's say you broke the Internet giving Quinn his first skating lesson."

"Huh?"

"Judy showed me a video."

"Strange, I didn't notice anyone we knew at the performance center."

"I'm not surprised; you're usually too focused on hockey anyway."

"I'm also uneasy with having videos of our son online no matter who posts them."

"You and Quinn interacting went viral."

"Oh shit."

Quinn fidgeted in his mother's arms. "Me see?"

Alex smiled and clutched him tighter. "Look, our son doesn't mind."

"All right, but no more pictures or videos of him on the Internet after today. You know how I feel about social media bullshit."

"Yes, encouraging you to have at least one verified account always falls on deaf ears."

"I deal with enough nut cases in person; I don't want Quinn growing up having all his business spread on the Internet."

"Yet you're the first one complaining how *I'm* overprotective of him."

"Don't start, Al."

"I'm making a point. Do you want to watch the video or not?"

"Mama, me go look!" Quinn cheered.

"Looks like I'm outnumbered," Troy replied. "I suppose one time won't kill me."

Alex gave him a knowing smile. "Get used to it, Papa; I have a feeling we'll see a lot more of Quinn on film in the future."

***

His father was the first goalie Quinn faced when he shot pucks at Troy in the basement of their Pittsburgh home. At three years old, Quinn already knew how to make blind passes and sometimes shot behind Troy, pucks slamming into a storage freezer.

Alex initially groused but grew acclimated to noises of father-son hockey "practices" and seeing dents on her freezer.

She made trips downstairs when curiosity about Quinn's progress overcame her, beaming with pride seeing him holding a miniature hockey stick as if it was second nature.

Another Troy in the making.

Quinn progressed into a proficient skater over the next year. The child's feet were always aligned and he never skated on his ankles. While children his age wobbled on the ice as they learned to skate, Quinn shot pucks off the boards.

His early skills didn't go unnoticed to anyone outside his family. He was chosen to play in locally sponsored midget leagues at four years old alongside boys five to six years older. Quinn was always smaller and younger than other kids on teams which he played, but both Troy and Parker assured him it was better to stand out as an undersized player.

Unlike other hockey dads, Troy refused to push his son hard as most other parents did. Seeing boys Quinn's age – and slightly older – run several miles following doing a two-hour workouts similar to one used by junior and professional-level players while trainers and parents bellowed like cruel drill sergeants aggravated Troy.

Do parents honestly think such brutality will turn their kids into the next AHC superstar? I'd rather shoot myself in the foot than put Quinn through the same kinds of hell.

Troy encouraged Quinn to prove he belonged on any team by working hard and not stressing about being perfect all the time.

"You'll have a long and difficult road ahead, especially with the Talmadge name. People will expect you to live up to the standards they demanded of me and your mother. Don't take comments made by fans and reporters seriously; they're only opinions. Go out on the ice, be yourself, and do what you do best: play the game."

Quinn took his father's advice to heart and "played the game" for years to come.

***

Chapter 3

Quinn was nine years old and Anna twelve when Alex became pregnant a fourth time. She and Troy were initially shocked; they didn't plan to have more children after Alex suffered a miscarriage when Quinn was three.

Alex's latest pregnancy thrilled and worried her. She figuratively walked on eggs the entire duration, bracing for further complications - or worse - another miscarriage.

Her anxieties were for moot; Noémie Louise Talmadge was healthy with petite features, a full head of ebony hair and her father's large dark eyes.

She was a perfect, placid baby who grew into a cheerful little girl with a constant smile and easily made friends. Unlike her older siblings, she showed no interest in hockey, finding joy in the world of horses and dreamed of being a veterinarian.

Anna and Quinn developed a strong bond with Noémie from the moment she came home.

Alex and Troy treasured their youngest child, taking Noémie and her siblings almost everywhere with them, including Rebels' practices and home games. Quinn loved propping Noémie on his lap, watching her fascinated expressions seeing Troy and his teammates on the ice. As his former mentor and boss Jon Halloran had done, Troy temporarily emerged from retirement so his children could see him play a final time.

Quinn loved his baby sister, but fondness of Noémie didn't stand in the way of his passion for hockey at a young age. He became so obsessed with the game during his entire stint at St. Rob's, teachers expressed concern to his parents.

"I attempted to distract Quinn with other activities but outside of occasional dabbling in photography, he only wanted to play hockey from the time Troy first put him in skates," Alex told a *Sports Weekly* writer years later. "Troy dismissed everyone's worries; he never understood the importance of Quinn developing additional interests and interacting with kids his own age."

Quinn's grades were far from affected by hockey; he maintained a straight-A average and aimed to become a role model to fellow students from his first day at St. Rob's, but his best friend, Phil O'Freel, knew the true Quinn Talmadge beneath his outward facade.

"Quinn wasn't an arrogant dumb jock like some of St. Rob's athletes," Phil said in the same *Sports Weekly* article. "He was shy and awkward throughout school but nice to everyone, especially kids in the special needs program and scholarship students. He didn't date much until sophomore year; the few times Quinn went to movies or school dances before meeting his first girlfriend, he'd take my sister. Otherwise, we'd hang out with other St. Rob's kids."

Tamar O'Freel elaborated on her twin brother's memory. "Quinn's parents and our dad [Marty] played for the Rebels before Dad signed with San Diego as a free agent. Phil and I grew up with their kids; I hit it off with Quinn first because I was a tomboy and we liked the same things. I accompanied him to dances and other social events at St. Rob's because he was too afraid to ask anyone else. No romance ever blossomed, but we've remained close friends."

The opposite sex fascinated Quinn from a distance but he remained shy around girls. Ironically, there were undoubtedly plenty of young ladies eager to date the St. Rob's hockey team captain.

"He wasn't confident away from the rink as everyone believed," Phil said. "He constantly joked about being funny-looking, but in reality, turned heads with his appearance from the time he turned fifteen."

"Anna teasing Quinn didn't help matters," Tamar replied. "I'd get irritated with her making fun of his 'ginormous hockey butt,' 'honking like a goose' when he laughed, his 'bowlegged waddle-walk,' or 'geeky driver's license picture looking like he wore a mullet.' Quinn blew off the comments, but I could the words hurt. I'd often remind him of girls at school who considered him cute to compensate for Anna's taunts."

Unbeknownst to Quinn and his closest friends, he'd already captured the interest of one girl in particular.

Her name was Chanel Jameson.

***

Chapter 4

"Dude, you landed the hottest girl in school." Connor Williams took a bite of his sandwich. "Cheerleader, volleyball team star, model, and TV spokesperson for Feldman Motors. At least let me in on your chick magnet secrets."

Quinn frowned. "How can I tell you when *I* don't know?"

"Oh, come on; you know you're a catch."

"What's so great about me?"

"Do we have to rehash the subject? You're an honor student, accomplished hockey player, National Merit Scholar, and an overall awesome person. How many times do I have to repeat the same shit? We're not going back to square one."

"Fine, but of all guys, I don't understand why someone like Chanel picked *me* to date."

"You over analyze everything, Quinn. I suggest you chill out and enjoy the moment. Has Chanel met your family?"

"She's coming for dinner Saturday. "

Connor gulped his soda and grinned. "I can't predict how your little sister and Alex will react, but Troy may love her."

"Dad's grateful I'm going places with a girl who isn't Tamar. Hey, do she or Lesley still have their world history notes? I need a copy since I missed class Monday for my dentist appointment."

"I'll have one of them to email you a copy, but you always manage getting A's though I rarely see you study."

"Mom and Dad always said I picked up things fast since I was a kid."

"Including hockey?"

"*Especially* hockey." Quinn rose from his seat. "I'd like to hang a bit longer, but I have AP English in ten minutes and promised Chanel I'd walk her to her math class beforehand."

***

"Are you looking forward to meeting Quinn's new girlfriend?" Alex asked. "I hear she's popular at school and he's always saying she's pretty."

Troy looked up from his computer. "I'm shocked Quinn found time for a girlfriend considering his hockey fixation."

"Sounds like someone else I know. Stella told me you seldom dated at his age."

"My mother seems to forget I attended three different schools, played in the Atlantic Canadian Junior Hockey League, and competed twice in Junior Internationals before age sixteen. Tamar's a great girl, but I'm glad Quinn is broadening his dating options."

"Me too."

"Did he mention anything else about Chanel, such as her parents?"

"Quinn says she's an only child and attending St. Rob's on full scholarship. Her father owns a little convenience store. Her mother does medical billing and coding from home."

"Sound like decent people."

"He met Chanel when she went to a game with her friends."

"My boy inherited the Talmadge charm."

"Don't get full of yourself," Alex kidded.

"I'm messing with you, Al. I don't think the world's sexiest women could divert our son's attention for long. He's too focused on hockey career goals."

Alex handed Troy a thin stack of paperwork. "Let's hope you're right. Guess we'll find out Saturday what kind of girl Chanel Jameson truly is."

***

"I never liked Chanel when we were cheerleaders at St. Rob's," Anna told Tamar during a phone call from Prague. "Something about her always bothered me."

"Know what you mean; I have an impression she's only with him for status or the Talmadge name."

"Exactly."

"Quinn's bringing her home Saturday."

Anna's voice dripped with sarcasm. "Great. I hope Troy and Mom see through her cutesy bullshit."

"Yeah, and she seems the slutty type. Quinn's far too good for her."

"To say the least, Tams. I hope my little brother knows what he's doing. I'd give Quinn the 411, but he'd call me a jealous bitch for my trouble."

"No use either of us wasting our breath. You know guys. By the way, how is your dad?"

Anna chuckled. "The usual Jax Ivanka; he never slows down. Who would've thought I'd go straight from graduating high school to playing for a team owned by my father? Mom was disappointed I didn't attend college first, but Dad says there's plenty of time."

"I read online he's dating someone new."

"Jesus, Tams, don't get me started. The so-called Finnish 'model' is only four years older than I am."

"Have you met her?"

"A couple times, but couldn't help but pick up a 'gold digger' vibes. Why else would she bother with Dad. He looks like a damn fool with Frida. Why couldn't he find a nice Czech woman his own age or at least another American like Mom? Aunt Jiva even makes fun of him."

"I'll guess the same reason Quinn hasn't drawn anyone who treasures him for his personality. Men sometimes think with the wrong head."

"*Sometimes?* Try 98 percent of their existence!"

"True."

"Keep me posted on Saturday's big event. *I* can't stand Chanel, but am curious what Mom and Troy have to say."

***

Chapter 5

Quinn and Chanel arrived on time Saturday evening. She was a tall, stunning blonde with perfect features and flawless skin. The girl seemed too worldly for sixteen, and Alex suspiciously eyed her any time Quinn turned his back.

"Something about her rubs me the wrong way," she said while Chanel used the bathroom.

Troy quizzically stared at her. "Al, aren't you being a little judgmental? Give the girl a chance."

Alex turned to Quinn. "Call it mother's intuition or whatever, but I don't get the impression she has a genuine interest in you as a person."

"Mom, try to be nice. I consider myself lucky to date someone like her."

"I'm sure there are far better girls who would love to go out with you."

"Did you talk to Anna and Tamar? I know neither likes Chan."

"I'm capable of forming my own opinions, Quinn. I don't think she's is the right one for you."

"You barely met her, Al," Troy interjected.

Alex darted annoyed glances at husband and son. "Both of you need to think with the organ between your ears more often. I'm going to check on dinner. Quinn, go find Noémie and tell her to help you and Francine set the table."

***

Seven-year-old Noémie Talmadge ambushed Chanel when she emerged from the bathroom. "Hi!"

Chanel gave her a wan smile. "Hello."

"I'm Noémie. Daddy and Quinn call me Pickle. Are you Quinn's girlfriend?"

"Um...yes."

"You're pretty."

"Thanks."

"Where you from?"

"Pittsburgh."

"Your dad a hockey player too?"

"No, he has a store and my mom does medical billing."

"I don't play hockey either. I have a horse. You want to see Blazing Fire?"

"Maybe later, okay?" *God, this kid is irritating.*

Quinn appeared in the doorway. "Pickle, quit interrogating Chan."

"I'm only saying hi. Jeez."

"Mom wants us to help Francine set the table." He turned to Chanel. "Sorry; my baby sister tends to be a chatterbox around new people."

She raised an eyebrow. *What took you so long?* "Noémie told me about her horse."

"Big surprise. Come on; let's go downstairs before Mom and Dad think we're doing something nasty."

I wish you would *do something 'nasty.'* Chanel managed a smile. "Sure, why not?"

***

Alex hoped against hope Quinn's fascination with Chanel hadn't gone far as them sleeping together. She couldn't believe her son was serious about the girl; the more she conversed with Chanel, the more Alex disapproved of her.

She grew uncomfortable with Quinn's behavior during dinner. Usually well-mannered and low-key, he now panted over Chanel at every opportunity. Alex gave Troy bemused looks, but neither he nor Noémie appeared fazed by Quinn's out-of-character antics.

Chanel, on the other hand, acted cool, leaning away from Quinn and barely accepted his arm around her. It became clear to Alex that Chanel had a high opinion of herself and was using their son for her own agenda. Nevertheless, Alex remained civil and polite as possible.

"Have you explored any post-secondary education or career options, Chanel?" she asked. "How about having a family someday?"

Chanel stared as if Alex had taken leave of her senses. "No. I have another year of high school and don't want kids."

"Too bad; I knew what I wanted to do at six years old, and Quinn's taking his SAT's next week."

"You guys didn't go to college and look how well you're doing."

Troy spoke up. "Hey, I took a couple of courses."

Alex hid a grin. "When you were twenty-seven."

"I got drafted by the AHC when I was barely out of high school."

He smiled in Chanel's direction. "While the possibility of Quinn following in my path seems likely, it's good for him to have backup plans."

"Oh?" Chanel stared at Quinn.

"I'm thinking either sports medicine or physical therapy if professional hockey doesn't work out," he replied.

"Pitt's among several schools that expressed interest in him," Alex said with pride.

"You want to waste four years going into debt with the possibility of having nothing to show for it?" Chanel asked Quinn.

He frowned. "We live in a city with some of the country's best hospitals. I could also open my own practice here or maybe Nova Scotia, but nothing's solid until I get my SAT scores and pick a school."

"Don't you want to keep playing hockey?"

"Sure, but having Dad's name doesn't mean an automatic guarantee for me to make it to the AHC or even on an elite Canadian team."

Noémie spoke up. "I'm not playing hockey. I'm going to be a vet and take care of horses like Dr. Mac does Blazing Fire."

"Better keep up your grades, Pickle," Troy replied with a smile. "Vet school's expensive and not everyone gets in."

"Okay, Dad, but I need help with math."

"Of course; you have to know what to charge people."

"Dr. Mac has somebody else make out his bills. He said I could work in his office on weekends when I'm older."

Alex gave her daughter an approving nod. "You'll gain experience which may help you get into a good school."

"Uh huh, that's what Dr. Mac said."

"See, Chanel? Noémie's seven and already knows what she wants to do."

Quinn glared at Alex. "Mom, both of us have plenty of time. You didn't bust Anna's chops as much and Chan gets enough shit at home."

"Language, young man; you aren't at hockey practice."

"Sorry. May we be excused? The movie starts in forty-five minutes."

"Put your plates in the dishwasher before you leave."

Troy tossed Quinn his key fob. "Take my Tesla, but no texting or talking on the phone while driving, mister. My insurance is already expensive without you having an accident over something stupid."

"All righty."

"Don't drive with a lead foot. There's a snow storm heading towards our area. If I much as see a scratch on the car or you get a traffic ticket, consider yourself grounded until end of school year."

"Yes, Dad." Quinn rolled his eyes.

"Be back by midnight," Alex said. "Anna's flight is due at nine tomorrow our time and you tend to be cranky in the mornings when you don't get enough sleep."

Quinn kissed her cheek. "See you guys around eleven-thirty."

***

Chapter 6

Alex closed the book she'd been reading when Troy came to bed. "I assume Quinn met his curfew."

He turned on the TV and flipped through several channels. "Yeah, barely ahead of the storm. Snow's coming down big time."

"Thank God. I don't care much for Chanel. She's too..." Alex's hand made a circling motion. "...self-absorbed and flighty."

"Jesus, Al. You need to dial back the bitchy helicopter mother act."

"Part of my job involves protecting our children's welfare."

"Quinn's no longer a frail baby near death. He'll likely make some choices you and I won't approve as he becomes a man. Nevertheless, we should be there for him."

"In other words, you're comfortable with him seeing that girl."

"I have no opinion one way or the other."

Alex gave him a teasing smile. "Shocking."

"Okay, Chanel's attractive and I'd probably hit on her in my day, but she has no direction. What kid doesn't have at least some idea what they want to do in life by her age?"

"Not everyone was born with a hockey stick in their hand, Troy."

"Funny. I had a backup plan in case hockey didn't materialize."

"Oh yes, the firefighter dream. Too bad you were afraid of heights. Quite a barrier for climbing 110-foot high ladders."

"I'm not scared of heights, Al. Good thing hockey worked out or I'd never met you and had amazing kids."

"I doubt you'd lacked for other potential wife material."

"Now you're trying to flatter me."

"Still humble after all these years."

"Strange as it sounds, I'd rather Quinn keep to himself instead of partying and posting half-naked pictures on social media like an asshole the way Connor Williams and Derek McCormick do. I doubt the O'Freel's would tolerate similar behavior from their kids."

"Especially Tamar; Marty rarely lets her out of his sight when she's not in school or at her games."

"Can't blame the man. Tamar's her daddy's girl."

"How well I know. Anyway, Quinn needs to concentrate on living his life and shouldn't get serious about any girl at the moment. Boys his age don't need to worry about getting attached. They should enjoy friends, get good educations, travel, make mistakes, and plan their futures."

"At least we can be comfortable knowing Quinn has primary and secondary goals. I don't think I've seen anyone more eager to take his SAT's."

"He hit the jackpot with Daddy's looks and brains."

Troy ran a hand up Alex's thigh and nuzzled her neck. "His mama's no imbecile either."

"Behave. Quinn's probably still awake and I'm cold. Did you forget to turn up the thermostat?"

"*I* can keep you warm all night long, baby."

"Go check the thermostat, Troy."

He groaned and got out of bed. "You're a pain in the ass."

"I love you too. Make sure the security alarm's also set. We don't need any surprise 'visitors' during the night."

***

Chapter 7

"No, honey, I understand," Alex said the following morning. "You're smart to reschedule with penalty fee waivers in effect. We can always talk on Skype or you can visit later this year."

Troy and Quinn entered the room. "Who's on the phone?"

"Anna. She changed her flight to another day since the storm caused so many to be canceled or delayed."

"Good move on her part," Troy said. "The Weather Channel said several East Coast airports are either closed or operating on limited basis."

"Pete Logan from the AHC also called. The Rebels-Presidents game scheduled in Washington tomorrow night is postponed until March 1."

"I figured. Storm pummeled DC big time. I'm sure our boys will welcome an extra off day."

The news irked Quinn. "You mean I dragged my ass out of bed for nothing? I could've slept another two hours!"

"Some things are out of our control, honey," Alex replied.

"Fuck it; I'll shoot pucks in the basement after breakfast."

"Language, mister."

"Dad curses all the time and you don't nag *him.*"

Troy sipped his coffee. "I can say otherwise, son."

Alex furrowed her brow. "Don't put dents on my new freezer. The warranty doesn't cover hockey puck damage."

Quinn studied his phone. "Sure, Mom."

"What did I tell you about no phone at the table?"

"I wanted to see if Chanel called or texted."

"I'm sure she can wait."

"Fine, whatever."

Noémie skipped into the room, delighted to have an unscheduled off day. "Hi guys!"

"Hey, Pickle," Troy greeted her. "You're in a good mood."

Quinn playfully ruffled Noémie's hair. "She's one of those annoying morning people."

She poked him. "Least I'm not grumpy like you."

"Good morning, sweetie." Alex set a full plate before her. "Any big plans today since you have no school?"

"When is Anna coming?"

"Not today, unfortunately. She rescheduled her flight."

"Aw, Mom! We haven't seen her forever."

"These things happen, honey," Alex said.

Troy nodded. "Better to cancel her plans than risk traveling in bad weather. Besides, Pickle, we can always catch up with her online."

"Yeah, but it isn't the same."

"Czech Mate said not long ago she wanted to come back the States. Damn, I hope that doesn't mean she's planning to quit the Capitals," Quinn said. "She's done an awesome job with them. I'd hate to see her throw away a promising future in hockey without another solid option in place."

"Doubt it; Jax would cut off his own foot before releasing her without a better offer in place. There are some AHC teams interested in drafting Anna, but Jax isn't the easiest guy to negotiate deals."

Troy sipped his coffee. "Isn't that the truth! Old Man always was a tough bastard."

Quinn excused himself. "I'll be in the basement if anyone needs me. Hey, Pickle, I could use a goalie. Are you up for the challenge?"

Noémie leaped from her chair. "Yeah! Can we go make a snowman after?"

"Whatever you wish, baby sis."

"What are you waiting for?" Noémie grinned at her brother. "Let's go have some fun!"

"Don't mess up my new freezer," Alex said to Quinn. "Dents from hockey pucks aren't covered in the warranty. Move the goal net to another spot if it isn't too much trouble."

***

Chapter 8

Chanel constantly nagged Quinn about taking her to St. Rob's junior prom as winter transitioned into spring.

"One night off from hockey won't kill you," she said. "Come on, all my friends are going."

"Jesus, Chan, you're a pain in the ass. I'm not big on school socials and need to stay sharp for the playoffs."

"Please, Quinnie? Don't be a loser."

"You knew how important hockey is for me for when we started seeing each another. You certainly never had problems hanging all over other guys, especially Jason Hooker."

"I'm dating *you* and your jealousy isn't flattering."

"I'm not jealous. Look, I need to get to class and have practice after school. Call you tonight?"

"Knock yourself out," Chanel snapped and stomped down the hall.

Quinn slammed his locker door, entered a nearby classroom, and sat at his desk. *Why does she always want to argue over petty shit?*

Connor slid into a chair beside him. "What's up, Cap?"

"Chanel's being a bitch."

"What else is new?"

"She's ridden my ass about junior prom since spring break ended."

"Whoa, whoa, whoa; wait a minute. You have a problem showing off your hot girlfriend?"

"We've only dated five months. The playoffs start in two weeks; last thing on my mind right now is some lame ass dance."

"One night away from hockey won't cause the world to end."

"Jesus, you sound like Chan."

"You gotta live, Cap. You'll have plenty of time to be a hockey geek. Isn't her birthday next week?"

"Yeah, I got her a locket. Why?"

"Give another gift by asking her to junior prom."

"Hmmm...maybe she'll finally shut up if I do."

Connor patted Quinn's shoulder and winked. "From what I've heard, perhaps more."

"What the hell do you mean?"

"Come on, Cap; it's legend Chanel Jameson banged a lot of dudes before she started dating you. Who's to say she doesn't have a few side pieces? You two haven't done anything besides hold hands, cuddle, and kiss."

"Relationships aren't only about sex, man."

"Whom you saving it for? If I was dating a smoke show like Chanel, we'd go at it at least three times a day."

Quinn scoffed. "You'd fuck anything breathing."

"I happen to enjoy banging hot babes. Sue me."

"I hope you're using rubbers or you'll be in deep shit if someone gets pregnant or you catch a disease from them."

"Do I look like a dumb ass? I never go on dates without at least half a dozen on hand. Better to be over prepared than not at all. Not everyone has your restraint, Cap."

"Shut up, Williams," Quinn snorted as their teacher entered the room.

***

Chapter 9

"Hey you," Chanel greeted Quinn when he approached her and a group of boys. "What's happening?"

He gave her a slight frown. *Jesus, I can't turn my back for a second and you're hanging with other guys.* "Funny, I was ready to ask the same question."

"Chatting with a few friends. Have you thought more about junior prom?"

"Don't start, Chan. Didn't I say we'd talk tonight?"

"Most guys would've asked before now."

"I prefer to get my priorities in order."

"Oh, I'm not among your so-called priorities?"

"Not what I meant, Chan. I need to get hockey playoffs and college interviews out of the way first."

Chanel snorted at him with impatience.

"I'll call you tonight," he said.

"Whatever. See you after class."

Quinn incredulously stared at her disappearing figure. *What the hell is with her hot and cold act? One minute she's lovey-dovey and the next a total bitch. One thing I do know: this commitment to one girl thing is a pain in the ass.*

Perhaps some insight from sort of an expert may help me...

***

Chapter 10

Quinn walked into his father's den after dinner that evening. "Dad, can we talk?"

Troy removed his glasses and put aside the paper he'd been reading. "Sure, take long as you need. Something go wrong at practice?"

"Practice went okay."

"Did you get in trouble?"

"No. I need some advice on...women."

"I'd usually say your mother's the better person for such a discussion, but I sense something more intense on your mind. Are you and Chanel still having problems?"

"I'm not sure. She's all over me like we hadn't seen each other in weeks and then practically bites off my head a moment later. I don't understand what I'm doing wrong."

"Don't be hard on yourself; things aren't always your fault. Now why are you and Chanel arguing?"

"She's irritating the shit out of me about junior prom and her timing is awful. Playoffs start next week, I need to get in much practice as possible, and I'm not big on school dances. Dragging me to the Holiday Ball last winter was bad enough."

Troy looked perplexed. "While I admire your competitive spirit and discipline, don't make the same mistakes I did. I all but shunned a social life at your age to get involved in sports and then got drafted. I had maybe two girlfriends my entire life and neither relationship lasted long at least until I met your mother. You're almost seventeen, Quinn; try to have fun once in a while."

"In other words, take Chan to junior prom?"

"Why not? I'll lend you one of my tuxes. Hanging out with some of your other teammates on occasion won't kill you either."

"I already go places with Phil, Connor, and Trevor."

"You should try expanding your horizons beyond childhood friends."

Quinn laughed. "Says the man who spent most of his younger years practically living in ice rinks. Grandma and Grandpa told me everything."

"Don't get smart. I'm only saying you won't be a teenager forever."

"Thanks for the advice, Dad. I promised to call Chan and discuss junior prom, so I better do it before she bends my ear again tomorrow at school."

***

Chapter 11

Alex fussed over Quinn on prom night, using a sticky roller to remove lint specks from his jacket, tugged various parts of his tuxedo, and put askew strands of hair back in place.

"Look at my baby," she cooed. "Troy! Come up and see our son."

"Be right there!" he yelled. "Let me grab my phone."

"Mom, chill out." Quinn grew irritated. "I have to pick up Chan soon."

"You have twenty minutes." She straightened his tie. "Since you borrowed your dad's tux, at least wear the thing right. Thank God it didn't need many alterations; you and he have the same build."

"Is it necessary for you guys to act like fools? I'm only going to prom, not a fucking royal wedding."

58

"Watch your language. Proms are among memorable milestones in a teenager's life that your dad and I never had chances to experience. Think of tonight as a trial run for senior prom next year."

"Whoa, who said anything about *senior* prom? I only agreed to go tonight so Chanel would shut her mouth."

Troy emerged from the basement. "Hey, looking good, buddy."

"Our baby's growing up fast," Alex replied.

"How about a couple shots?" Troy asked.

Quinn sighed in resignation. "Make it quick, Dad. I'm already nervous and don't want tonight getting off on the wrong foot."

"Don't worry, you'll be fine."

Alex withdrew to the kitchen. "I'll leave you two men alone."

"Where's Pickle?" Troy asked.

"I told you this morning she's staying overnight at Tessa's, remember?"

"Oh...right."

He took several pictures before Quinn stopped him. "I have to go, Dad. Chan will be pissed if I'm late."

Troy gave him a quick hug, dug in his pocket, and slipped a small item into Quinn's hand with a wink. "Have a good time. Here's a little something for later."

Quinn gasped at the sight of a condom. *"Dad!"*

"Do you think since I never attended a prom I don't know what happens afterward? Always be prepared."

"Chan and I never slept together...yet."

"Sometimes things get hot and heavy on prom night."

"I can't believe we're having this conversation."

"Every boy should have one with their old man."

Quinn rolled his eyes. "Goodbye, Dad."

Alex returned to the living room and pecked Quinn's cheek. "Have a good time, honey. Stay safe and call if you need anything."

"Thanks for everything. Don't wait up, guys."

"I'll be long asleep," Troy replied, "but guarantee Mama stays awake long as possible until you're home. Don't say you weren't warned."

***

Chapter 12

Quinn's best friend Phil O'Freel spotted him at the punch bowl. "Dude, what are you doing? I figured you and Chanel would be living it up on the dance floor."

"Who are you to criticize? You brought your own sister."

"Michelle blew me off for some basketball lunk and Tam-Tam's guy no-showed. Dad spent serious money on stuff for prom and gotten his Irish up big time if I didn't bring her."

"Are you kidding me?"

"I wish. Tam-Tam and Dad were pissed. I honestly think he scared off the dude so I could keep an eye on her."

"Doesn't surprise me. I can't remember a time Marty hasn't been protective of Tams."

"Seriously, why aren't you hanging with Chanel?"

"She's too busy playing social butterfly and I suck at dancing. Sometimes I think I'm less of an actual boyfriend and more a prize to show off to her snotty friends."

"Women, a species I'll never understand."

"You and me both, Phil. I didn't want to come to this stupid thing in the first place."

Connor sidled up beside them. "What's up, dudes?"

Quinn took a couple whiffs and glared. "Getting the after prom festivities started early, Williams?"

"I had a couple pre-festivities drinks. Lesley didn't give a shit."

"You better pray to God none of the chaperones smell that shit on you," Phil said.

"News flash, big guy; St. Cloud, his girl, his little sister, and the Cap's babe are also out back sampling the party favors."

"Christ, Williams!" Quinn exclaimed. "Are you morons trying to get kicked off the team before our championship game?"

"Lighten up, Cap; I only had two beers."

"You, Phil, and Trevor are the team's best defesemen and we can't afford to lose any of you. Go find a breath mint, get your shit together, and bring Trevor's ass back inside."

"Yes, *Dad,*" Connor sarcastically replied.

"I mean it, Williams. You and he better not fuck up this championship opportunity for the rest of us."

Chanel spotted Quinn and grabbed him in a tight hug. "Here's my Quinnie hermit!"

He turned up his nose at the smell of her breath. "Chan, have you been drinking?"

"Only a few sips, baby."

"A few sips my ass. You smell like a wine bar."

"You're lame!" She tugged his jacket sleeve. "Come on, Quinnie, let's dance."

"You can barely stand as it is. Sit down and I'll get us some punch."

"I don't need punch. Stop being a bore."

"See, things like your present attitude's one reason I did not want to come tonight. I could've spent time at home practicing for the playoffs."

Chanel dismissed him with a wave of her hand. "Fine, I'll find someone else to dance with."

"More like give you free booze. Aren't you worried about being caught?"

"What do you care? All you want to do is either play stupid hockey or hang out with your goofy friends and annoying sister."

"Don't talk shit about Pickle; she's only a kid. This is the first time St. Rob's boys team made the playoffs in over ten years. How can you say hockey is 'stupid'?"

Chanel rose from her chair. "I'm going to say hi to Jason and Oscar."

"I'm sure they'll have more in mind."

"Are you calling me a slut?"

"If the shoe fits..."

"Ugh! Go home, Quinn; I'll find another ride. I'm sick of your jealous bullshit."

"Then don't come whining to me if you get a disease or knocked up, you fucking skank."

Chanel picked up a nearby object and hurled it at him. "Get out! We're done! I wish I never bothered with you in the first place."

***

Chapter 13

Chanel's junior prom breakup with Quinn marked the beginning of what he viewed as his life falling apart.

After a strong playoff start, St. Rob's lost the final championship round to their crosstown rivals, St. Thomasina, when Trevor St. Cloud missed a goal that could've tied the game and send it into overtime.

Quinn blamed himself for the team's devastating loss, often questioning his capabilities as captain. Quinn and Trevor were close friends, and he felt responsible for the backlash Trevor received weeks afterward.

His heart still stung from both the game's unfortunate end and breaking up with Chanel; while she often drove him nuts about trivial things and they often argued, Quinn had still cared about her. He spent the following weeks moping in his room, only leaving for meals and school.

"I'm done with women," he told Phil in a text message . "To be honest, I want to drop out of life in general."

"Damn, Quinn, please tell me you aren't considering doing something stupid."

"I fucked up two opportunities. Maybe I should ghost for a while."

"No chick is worth that, man. Chanel may be the hottest girl in school, but she'd been banging Jason behind your back the entire time you two were supposedly serious. Why do you think Daria wanted to kick her ass before finally having enough sense to dump him? Jason and Chanel deserve each other. They're both ho-bags."

"The championship..."

"Losing wasn't your fault or anyone else's! *Trevor* missed that goal and you took it harder than he did. People still give him shit. but he's already moved on to be better next season."

"My soul is so dark...it's like someone reached inside and turned off the lights."

"Don't make me tell your parents or send over Dad to knock some sense into you."

"I'm not going to try anything, Phil. I only want to be alone for a while."

"Good to hear, man. Besides, only a few weeks of school remain, and then you'll head to Nova Scotia. Maybe you'll meet someone nice in Yarmouth. I've always heard good stuff about Canadian girls."

"Didn't I say earlier that I'm done with women?" Quinn asked.

"Dude, you'll be seventeen in a couple months. Plenty of girls out there wanting a catch like you. Quit selling yourself short."

"Says the guy who seldom has them beating down *his* door and took his sister to junior prom."

"Weird-looking ginger dudes like me don't exactly top lists of girls' dream dates."

"Even a top-notch defenseman? Your dad obviously had few problems getting women."

"Sure, if you count his banging endless parades of puck bunnies in Pittsburgh and San Diego before meeting Mom. Nana Mo said Dad fell in love the moment they met. He's proof that even gargoyles eventually pull decent chicks."

"Kind of helps when some gargoyles are worth $20 million."

"Mom never cared about Dad's money or social status. She didn't bother watching any sports before they met. Look how things worked out for *your* parents; of all the world's hottest women who wanted to get into his jock, Troy chose to steal your mom from Jax Ivanka."

"Uhhh, my parents already had kind of a thing going before Mom married Mr. Ivanka."

"Yet Troy won her back. Life isn't hopeless as you think, man."

"Could have fooled me."

"Christ, you're a downer. At least make the effort to stop pitying yourself long enough to attend Noémie's horse show on Saturday."

"Don't worry, Mom will find a way to drag my ass there. She's done nothing but nag me to do other shit for the last several weeks."

"What are you doing tonight? I need a study buddy for the Earth Science final scheduled on Monday."

"Why not ask Tams?"

"She's already charmed some Latino kid from the swim team. Don't ask me how."

"Ginger women fascinate some guys. Sure, come on over; it's not like I have anything better to do than listen to Mom bitch about me rarely leaving the house."

"See you after dinner. Maybe we can hang out in your basement and shoot a few pucks afterward. Never too soon to gear up for next season."

"Sounds good to me. God knows we need any and all help possible."

***

Chapter 14

"Tomas," **Tamar snapped** at her study partner, "I thought you agreed to us studying with Phil and Quinn. Stop texting your hoochies; it's rude."

"I'm not texting a hoochie," he replied. "Needed to tell my parents you and I at Quinn's house."

"See, there's one example of why you can't keep a man," Phil teased.

"Fuck you, Phil."

"Not possible, little sister."

"You're only seven minutes older, jagoff."

"Can we get to the next chapter?" Quinn asked. "You two complain about me not doing anything or going out yet when I do have anyone over, they want to goof off."

"Wow," Tamar said, "and you talk about *girls* being moody. Are you still brooding about Chanel?"

"None of your business."

Tomas brightened. "Ooooh, Chanel. *Hermosa niña.*"

Tamar glared at him. "Yeah, beautiful girl and St. Rob's biggest slut." She punched his arm. "Anyone who sleeps with half the basketball team while dating Quinn needs their head examined. Typical scholarship trash, that one."

"Jesus, why not twist the knife, Tam-Tam?" Phil said.

"Sorry, but it's true."

"While I agree she's an easy lay, not all scholarship kids are trash."

Quinn nodded at his best friend. "A girl in one of my AP classes is on scholarship. I borrowed her notes a couple times."

"Is she hot?" Tomas asked.

"What makes the difference?"

"You'll eventually need to find someone in your league, holmes."

"I'm not looking for another girlfriend. I have enough damn problems."

Tamar wrinkled her nose. "Ew, don't tell me you still have feelings for Chanel."

"Maybe."

"You need help, Quinn. There are far better girls in school than that whore."

"Kill the snotty commentary and help us study, Tams." He picked up a book and flipped several pages. "This Earth Science final isn't going to pass itself."

***

Chapter 15

Quinn and his family traveled to Yarmouth as they did each summer when the school year ended. He was grateful for the change in scenery; Pittsburgh still held painful memories of the last few months.

Summer in Nova Scotia allowed Quinn little time for moping. Strength and conditioning coach Bill Fontana worked with Quinn building exceptional core strength since his young client was thirteen years old.

Fontana specialized in hockey-related biomechanical and neurological efficiency; 90 minutes running track, weight training another 90 minutes, and then 45 minutes targeted muscle work between appropriate recovery periods. Quinn aimed to be the best, and Fontana encouraged every effort to sharpen his skills.

On days he didn't work with Fontana, Quinn spent hours training solo, concentrating on a skill to emerge from remaining completely still to accelerating to 25 mph as Troy did many times during his own career quite accomplished feats by bowlegged father and son.

Alex was happy to see Quinn's main passion keeping him occupied in contrast to constantly brooding, but the near-lack of his participation in summer activities most seventeen-year-old boys enjoyed still perturbed her.

"Damn, Al," Troy said when she expressed her concerns. "You complained when Quinn hung around the house feeling sorry for himself, now you're worried he's spending 'too much time' training with Bill or practicing in the basement?"

"School's out, Troy. He should enjoy at least part of our summer vacation. Noémie takes time away from horse shows and riding lessons when she's not in school."

"Pickle's eight years old and not being considered for athletic scholarships. Quinn's done other things while we've been in Yarmouth, by the way."

"Golfing with you and visiting your parents don't exactly qualify. We have a nice pool; he could have over some friends, do some fishing or race his jet ski at the lake. Boys his age usually-"

"We both know Quinn isn't like most his peers, Al, no matter how much you try to mold him."

"He could at least visit one of the local hangouts with friends and maybe meet girls."

Troy scoffed. "Are you serious? He rarely brings any home and the few times it happens, you find some reason to dislike each girl."

"No I don't."

"Bullshit; you always make snide remarks when they aren't in the room."

"I can easily spot gold diggers and users, Troy. You saw what effect that despicable Chanel had on Quinn, especially after she broke up with him during prom. I knew something was off from the beginning when Noémie didn't like her, and that child loves *everyone*."

"She wasn't his ideal match, big deal. He'll only be seventeen in a couple weeks and has plenty of time to find the right girl."

"Quinn has been an old man in a boy's body long as either of us remembers. He deserves a young woman who appreciates his maturity instead of viewing it as a liability."

"Not to mention she's willing to learn all things hockey."

"Passion for the game would be a bonus long as she wasn't some disgraceful puck bunny."

"Those women are easy to spot, so I can't see Quinn getting fooled."

"You're right, Al. He's a smart kid."

"A modern version of you." Alex flashed Troy a smile. "We're lucky to have a son who's more content golfing with his father and playing tennis with his baby sister than having orgies with women pouring vodka on his chest or sleeping with a yoga wear sales girl almost young enough to be his daughter."

Troy burst into laughter. "Damn, woman, you're brutal. Can't resist digs on Claude Caldwell and Marty, can you?"

"The first pair to immediately pop into my mind. Thank God Marty settled down after he met Harper."

"The right woman tends to have a positive effect on men."

"You can add my ex-husband to the list of athletes gone wild. Or in Jax's case, completely lost his mind."

"Is Old Man still with that Finnish model?"

"Yes, and they're engaged. Anna's not thrilled, to put it mildly."

"I wouldn't be doing cartwheels either. How is she aside from dealing with his antics?"

"Great. She's considering retirement from the Prague Capitals and returning to America."

"Old Man will have a fucking stroke."

"Anna's a grown woman so he'll adjust. She's expressed interest in either training or coaching."

"That's fantastic! I can introduce her to some key people when she's ready."

The front door slammed. "Mom!" Quinn called. "Is there any lemonade left? Pickle and I are parched!"

"I made a fresh pitcher this morning, honey," Alex said. "Did you have a nice game?"

Noémie skipped into the room. "We had fun!"

Quinn poured four glasses of lemonade with a grin. "Speak for yourself, Pickle."

"I beat him three times," Noémie said.

"Because I let you," he teased her.

"No way! I won fair and square."

Quinn handed Noémie a glass and ruffled her hair. "You sure did, kiddo."

Alex gave Troy a knowing look. "Glad to see one of my men isn't a total sore loser."

"You're hilarious," he replied and took a sip of lemonade.

"Winning's fun, Dad," Quinn said, "but we can't do it all the time. If we're always on top, what's left to work towards? That's what Grandpa always tells me."

"Try thinking like that once you hit the pros, boy," Troy said. "Now there's where you'll have some *serious* competition."

***

Chapter 16

"Quinn, put away your phone," Alex said. "You've been on the thing for hours. What's so important that you're wasting a beautiful day?"

"Phil's texting a bunch of suggestions on how the team can improve next year. No one wants a repeat of what happened in the championship final against St. Thomasina."

"Shouldn't that be your coach's job?"

"Yeah, but I'm captain and need to up my leadership skills. No one said anything out loud, but I can't help but wonder if they too came into question."

"Why keep rehashing everything? The season and school year have long ended."

"Dad obsessed about losing to San Diego in the Princeton Trophy final for over a year and no one said boo. How's that any different from what I've had to endure?"

"The media blasting him and Marty gloating didn't help matters."

"What sucked the most was it being Dad's last playing season. Talk about finishing one's on-ice career on a low note. He *hates* losing."

"No one enjoys losses but if anyone had to retire under less than ideal circumstances, it was Marty."

"He had one nasty injury after being slammed into the boards and losing his helmet."

"Much as his constantly heckling your dad after the San Diego win irritated me, we were both thankful Marty didn't have a worse outcome."

"That injury apparently didn't incapacitate him too much. Harper got pregnant not long afterward."

Alex crossed her arms and glared. *"Quinn Parker Talmadge."*

"What? Phil jokes about his parents' quickie wedding all the time."

"Still not funny. Marty stepped up and accepted responsibility, something not many men do these days."

"He's a lucky dude, Mom. I wish I could find someone like you and her. All I've gotten are cheating bitches and bimbos who only want to brag about dating a Talmadge."

"You'll meet a nice girl when the time comes, honey. What else did you accomplish today?"

"Shooting some pucks in the basement. Pickle makes a great goalie. I think she's missing her true calling."

"Noémie's probably the only Talmadge who's *doesn't* want to pursue a hockey career no matter how good everyone says she is. She enjoys competing in horse shows too much."

"She'll make a good vet someday too. Lots of people and animals are drawn to her."

"Well, she's a bubbly little girl who's hard not to love."

"True." Quinn grew quiet for a few moments. "Mom?"

"What, honey?"

"Will I ever to make it to the pros like you and Dad?"

"I honestly don't know since I didn't exactly enter the AHC in traditional fashion. That's something you need to discuss with your father. I can say lots of top-notch players never see a day in the AHC or any other professional organization, but you have an incredible talent for the game. Many quality colleges are all but tripping over one another to offer you athletic scholarships. Who knows, college hockey could be a first step in the right direction."

"Crazy you mentioned college. Phil said he was offered a full athletic scholarship to the same university Marty went."

"Really? Neither Marty nor Harper mentioned anything; then again, I haven't spoken to them since we left Pittsburgh. Did Phil say anything about Tamar? Now *there's* an outstanding goaltender. You should incorporate her into some of your basement practices instead of using Noémie or your grandmother all the time."

"I'll think about it when school starts. Too bad Tams isn't allowed to play with the guys, which I think is bullshit. Women now play in the AHC thanks to you. Why not have co-ed high school and college teams?"

"I'm sure Tamar is content helping the girls win another championship."

"Least they got one. Talk about making us guys look like assholes."

"Don't start, Quinn."

"I can't help it. All I see is Trevor missing the goal."

"Which he's likely long over. Your team will have another shot."

"Mooooooooooooooooooommmmm!" Noémie called. "Anna's on Skype and she has big news!"

"We'll be right there," Alex replied. "Can you get your dad? He's probably in his man cave or the den."

"You go ahead, Mom," Quinn said. "I'll catch up in a few."

***

Chapter 17

"Long time since we heard from you, young lady," Troy said. "We were starting to wonder if something happened."

"Sorry for worrying everyone and not having time to arrange another visit," Anna replied. "Dad's kept me busy since the Capitals' season ended."

"He always was a workhorse."

"Are you sure everything's all right?" Alex asked.

"Things couldn't be better, Mom. I wanted to catch up with you guys while I had the chance."

"Pickle said you had big news," Troy said.

Noémie leaned closer to the computer screen. "Yeah, are you coming to see us?"

Anna laughed. "You could say that's among my plans in the near future."

"Wow! When?"

"Pickle, let your sister talk," Troy gently chided her.

"Don't be hard on her," Anna said. "She's excited to see me."

Noémie gave her a bright smile. "I am."

"Where's Quinn?"

"Upstairs. I'll miss the big news since I have to go to my riding lesson."

"I'm sure the others will keep you up to speed."

"Yeah. See you later, Anna."

"Bye, Pickle. Have fun."

"Quinn will be here in a few minutes," Alex said. "We had a mother-son chat earlier."

"Please say he's over the breakup from Chanel."

"Yes, but still blames himself for St. Rob's losing the boy's hockey team championship. Quinn has his father's mentality; it's automatically his fault when anything goes wrong."

"Hey," Troy interjected. "Captains shoulder a lot of responsibility. Take it from a man who knows."

Quinn entered the room with a grin. "Damn, are you all still talking about me?"

Anna waved at him onscreen. "There's my favorite baby brother!"

"Hey, Czech Mate," he greeted her. "Glad to know you're still alive."

"Dad's been working me like crazy."

Troy steered the conversation back to its original intention. "What's the news you wanted to share?""

"For starters, I'm coming back to America soon," Anna said.

"Honey, that's wonderful!" Alex replied. "When?"

"I'm planning a temporary stop in Pittsburgh, but my return in general is permanent. I retired from the Capitals."

Anna's revelation stunned Alex. "You finally made the leap?"

"Yes. I decided to hang up the skates and explore other options on my own instead of being forced like Dad was when he blew out his knee."

"I'm surprised he went along with the idea."

"Makes two of us," Troy said.

"Dad has no choice," Anna replied. "The San Diego Pacific hired me as their skating coach."

"Congratulations! When do you start?"

"I'm due to report in two weeks, so a possible side visit may be short."

"The Pacific isn't wasting any time."

"Sounds like a challenging job," Quinn said.

"I wouldn't have accepted otherwise, little brother."

Quinn turned to his parents. "You should tell Marty the news."

Alex smiled. "Good idea."

"No way!" Troy protested. "Last thing we need is Marty having more ammunition to bust my chops. He can read the news online like everyone else."

Alex sighed. "For God's sake, bringing him back to Pittsburgh as assistant coach was *your* bright idea."

"You and Marty always chirped at each other long as anyone remembers, Dad," Quinn added.

"You have a point. Anyway, good luck with your new job, Anna."

"Thanks," she said. "Now that I revealed the first part of my news, I have something else."

"What?" Alex asked.

"I'm not coming back to America alone."

"Oh God, don't tell me your dad insists on accompanying you."

"No, he's staying here with Frida. He doesn't visit America these days any more than he has to."

"Then who...?"

"Mom, I'm engaged!"

"To whom? We had no idea you were dating anyone."

"Congrats, Czech Mate," Quinn said. "Who's the unfortunate victim caught in your web?"

"Funny, little brother," Anna replied. "His name's Jiri Stratka and we met following a Capitals game five months ago. He owns a box suite at the arena."

"How old is he? What does he do for a living?" Alex asked. "Does his family know about your engagement?"

"Whoa, Mom; slow down. Jiri's parents were killed in an accident when he was six and his grandmother raised him. She died two years ago."

"Sorry to hear he no longer has any family."

"Jiri was long used to being alone when we met. He's thirty and an executive for a company dealing in – of all things – equipment for professional hockey teams. They have offices all over the world, so he had no problem having his transfer to San Diego granted."

"Thirty?" Troy asked. "Isn't he a little...?"

"Don't *you* start, Troy," Anna scolded him. "I've already gotten enough aggravation from my hypocrite father. Dad's marrying a woman not much older than I am, yet has balls to bitch about the ten-year age difference between me and Jiri."

"I guess it's safe to say Old Man isn't excited about your engagement."

"Ha! That's putting it mildly. Dad won't give Jiri a chance, but if I have to tolerate Frida as my stepmother, he'll have to suck it up having Jiri for a son-in-law."

"Ten years aren't bad," Alex said. "Your father should count his blessings you didn't settle for some useless bum like Terrell Johnson."

"Yeah, talk about dodging a bullet. That taught me a lesson about slumming with public school boys. Did I mention your future son-in-law was among Prague's most eligible bachelors before we met?"

"Sounds like you landed quite a catch. We can't wait to meet Jiri."

"Dad and I could use another man in the family," Quinn said. "When's your wedding?"

"We want to settle in San Diego before picking a date. Jiri's enrolled in an English as second language class. He's doing so well, he'll be fluent before anyone knows it. My speaking to him in mostly English helps."

"When do you plan to stop in Pittsburgh?" Alex asked. "I'll prepare your old room for anything you and Jiri need."

"Oh, Mom, that isn't necessary."

"Getting extra things won't be a problem," Troy added. "No way are my stepdaughter and her fiance staying in a hotel when we have plenty of room for both of you."

Quinn beamed. "Not to mention all the money you'd save on room service and the honor bar. Nobody can beat Mom's home cooking."

"Let me guess," Anna said in an amused tone. "You want to recruit Jiri as a goalie for basement hockey practice."

"Wouldn't hurt; he'd make a great change from Pickle and Grandma."

"You're in luck. Jiri used to be a goaltender for one of the Czech Republic's junior leagues."

Quinn let go an impressed whistle. "No way! I haven't met the dude and already like him. Why did he quit playing?"

"Not everyone lives and breathes hockey like some people," Anna replied with a laugh. "Jiri found his niche away from the ice, but occasionally indulges in pond hockey for fun."

"You two should visit during Christmas break. He and I could challenge each other on the O'Freel's back pond, that is if he can handle our cold weather."

"Try spending one winter in Prague. I think Jiri would have few problems handling Pittsburgh in December."

"Man, it will be great having a brother figure. Not that I don't love you and Pickle, but..."

"I get it, Quinn. Anyway, guys, time for me to log off. I was due at Dad's ten minutes ago and surprised he hasn't yet sent out a search party."

"Don't be a stranger," Troy said, "We'd like to hear from you more often."

"I can't guarantee anything before the move to San Diego, but I'll try to stay in touch."

"At least drop an email on occasion," Alex replied.

"I'll do my best, Mom. In the meanwhile, Quinn, you promise me you'll stop driving Mom and Troy crazy with the 'woe is me' act. A new school year is around the corner and it's time for you to focus on the fun that comes with senior year. No more dwelling in the past, okay?"

"I don't think you'll need to worry anymore, Czech Mate." Quinn sported a wide smile. "Hearing from you makes me feel much better!"

***

Chapter 18

Quinn entered his final year at St. Rob's with a more lighthearted demeanor; he looked forward to Anna's wedding and enjoyed hearing about her new job with the San Diego Pacific. Each of her emails detailed jocular anecdotes about working with the Pacific's roster, making Quinn howl with laughter.

"Nice to see the old Talmadge," Phil said on their first day of school. "Guess I don't need to ask how your summer in Yarmouth went."

"Summer started kind of meh," Quinn replied, "but then kicked ass after we heard from Anna!"

"Dad mentioned her new gig in San Diego. You must be excited as hell for her, man."

"You betcha. I'm also gaining a brother-in-law."

"Wait! Anna's getting married? Damn, there goes my chance with her."

"You never had one anyway, bro. She and her fiance haven't set a date. She's seeking wedding advice from Mom, but Mr. Ivanka's still mad."

"Who pissed in his canteen?" Phil asked.

"Mr. Ivanka's not thrilled about the age difference between Anna and her fiance. Getting drunk at her dad's wedding before she and Jiri left for San Diego didn't help matters."

"I would've done some serious drinking too. What's her fiance like? Have you met him?"

"No, but Jiri sounds cool. He was a goalie in juniors years ago and currently an executive in pro hockey equipment sales. He kept his home in Prague in addition to the one he and Anna bought in San Diego. She wanted to stop in Pittsburgh before Pickle and I went back to school, but the Pacific's GM needed her to start soon as possible. She and Jiri are planning to visit either at Christmas or during the All-Star break."

"You're right, I wouldn't have had a chance with Anna," Phil said with a grin. "How could I compete with a big shot like him?"

"Don't worry, man; there's still some chance of getting a brother-in-law of your own."

"Not while Dad's still breathing. I swear he wants to lock up Tam-Tam until she's fifty. You're the only guy he's never bitched about taking her anywhere."

"We go out as *friends,* Phil. I'm not officially dating your sister and been done with women since Chanel dumped me."

"So you say."

"Anyway, how was your summer?"

Phil scoffed. "Most of it was spent at Dad's cabin in the middle of bum fuck nowhere Missouri. *You* tell *me.*"

"Huh? I heard his cabin is awesome and the lake a great place for boating."

"Then you go there next summer while Tam-Tam and I spend time with your family in Yarmouth. Mom must still be madly in love with Dad to deal with his 'I may be a former AHC player but still a good old Missouri boy' bullshit. She's usually the type that's happier staying at Motel 6 than some lame ass cabin with the nearest cell phone reception thirty minutes away."

"Love makes people do things out of the box, my man."

"Do you have an idea when our first hockey team practice begins? Tam-Tam said the girls start Monday after school."

Quinn shook his head. "I haven't talked to anyone yet."

"By the way, my aunts are planning to attend some of our games this year," Phil said.

"Oh God, please don't expose me to your Aunt Maeve. I can deal with Anne Marie, but-"

"Maeve loves the idea of you going down. All good-natured teasing, least according to her. I think she actually enjoys finding ways to piss off Dad."

"Explains why she's always yelling catcalls when I do important plays."

"If it helps, Maeve did the same to Dad when he played in college and then his first professional games in New Jersey. Hell, she even busts my balls on occasion, yet Tam-Tam gets a free pass."

"Women stick together," Quinn said. "Seriously, though, we all need to crack down and work harder this year if we're going to have another playoff shot. I don't want another repeat of last year's nightmare against St. Thomasina. I hear they're still bragging about beating us for the championship."

"I'm on board, but you need to let shit go. Trevor trained like a champion all summer. Look for our man to come back strong. Connor worked out more often during the summer and he's one of our biggest goof-offs. I think losing could benefit everyone in the long run, least long as no one's seriously injured this season."

"Christ, I hope so."

"That loss could be motivation we need to aim towards bigger and better things. If my ass got a full scholarship to U of Missouri, great things can definitely happen to some of the other guys, particularly you. Mark my words, bro, this will be our year."

***

Chapter 19

Maeve O'Freel-Clinton stood behind the glass constantly heckling Quinn during the St. Rob's boys hockey team's season opener. "You little asshole," she yelled before a face off in the opponents' zone. "Overrated brat who only earned his 'C' because who Daddy is."

Marty shot his older sister a dirty look. "What the hell are you doing? We're at a high school game for Christ's sake. Take it down a dozen notches."

"Someone needs to put that snot-nosed kid in his place," she replied. "Come on, it's all in good fun."

"Tormenting a boy barely seventeen years old and calling him vile names isn't my idea of fun. Quinn's an outstanding player, busted ass, and earned everything on his own merit."

"Keep telling yourself that, Marty."

"Sit down, be quiet, and watch the game. No wonder Allan rarely takes you anywhere. You're lucky Troy made an emergency trip to the john or he would smack you into next week."

"Bullshit, he's much a wimp as his son. Where are Harper, Tamar, and Alex? I thought they enjoyed coming to the boys' games."

"Tamar's grounded for missing curfew last night and Harper's at home with her. Alex is working concession and she can see everything fine when the stand isn't busy. Now am I asking too much wanting to watch this game in peace?"

Maeve sat and sulked. "To think you used to be the fun brother."

"Hush, here's another face-off."

Quinn often won face-offs and set up his opponent for a slap shot near the blue line, but tonight was an exception. He took possession when the puck dropped and scored within four seconds. The red goal light flashed and Quinn turned, faced Maeve with a mocking grin, and saluted her.

"Smug little shit," she muttered while Marty laughed.

Troy returned to his seat. "What happened? I heard everyone go nuts on my way back from the rest room."

"You should skip Taco Bell stops before games, boss," Marty said. "Quinn scored seconds after the face-off."

"Shit, my rotten luck to miss it."

"I captured everything on my phone. Want to take a look? Quinn saluted my dear sister after his goal."

Troy chuckled and turned to Maeve. "You'll never learn when to stop heckling the boy, will you?"

She shot him a dirty look. "Not my fault some people can't handle a little jovial taunting."

"Jovial?" Marty asked while watching the on-ice action. "Try vicious."

He then leaped from his seat and pounded on the glass in anger after Phil received a penalty. "That's his own stick! Kid lifted Phil's stick! He lifted that stick right at Phil, you asshole ref!"

"God, stop acting like Phil got ejected," Maeve said. "He only has a two-minute penalty."

"The other little bastard lifted that stick, yet *Phil* gets nabbed for high sticking? These zebras suck ass."

"Don't get your Irish up, Marty," Troy said. "He'll be fine."

As predicted, Phil charged from the penalty box once the two-minute penalty expired and waved to his father.

Marty waved back with a grin. "Show off."

"Phil acts more like his old man more each day," Troy replied.

"Oh come on! I was never that bad."

"Right. I suppose cussing out the ref during one of the last games you played after sending pucks over the glass *twice* qualified as calm and collected."

"That son of a bitch zebra acted like I did it on purpose. Besides, you've given refs more earfuls than anyone could count."

"Another tough job of being team captain."

"Whatever. At least I finally got a Princeton Trophy win with the Pacific, so fuck you."

"You were injured and didn't play in Game Six, asshole."

"Rather hard to play after getting a good smack in the head." Marty spotted Phil attempt a goal. "Come on, boy...come on, boy! Shoot it, Phil! Capitalize on Quinn's pass! Middle, Phil, middle!"

"Perfect!" Troy said when Phil scored and the crowd around them cheered.

Marty leaped from his seat. "Yeaaaaaaaaaaaaaaah! Way to move! Good shot into the net. Heavy, son! Heavy!"

An opponent shoved Quinn to the ice after his and Phil's goal celebration, a move missed by the referee.

"Oh hell no!" Troy bellowed. "Are you fucking blind, ref? Put that other kid in the penalty box for unsportsmanlike conduct!"

"Zebras must be taking lessons from AHC refs," Marty said. "Funny how they missed Quinn getting shoved yet busted Phil for allegedly high-sticking."

Troy nodded in agreement. "I'd swear someone bet serious money on St. Therese's team if I didn't know any better."

"Either that or another attempt to hurt Quinn. There's always at least one jerk that enjoys taking cheap shots at him."

"He can always take a dive or two like his father used to," Maeve quipped. "Isn't that what you did in your playing days, Troy?"

He and Marty shot her death stares.

"What?" she asked.

"Jokes about Troy 'diving' weren't funny in 2005, let alone the present," Marty hissed in her ear. "For Christ's sake, Maeve, he's been my boss and friend since before the kids were born. Is asking to *not* embarrass me and Phil in front of Troy an unreasonable request?"

Maeve huffed and slouched in her seat without another word.

"Nice one, buddy! Great job!" Troy cried when Quinn blasted the puck past St. Therese's goaltender with ease.

"What happened? Did I miss something?" Marty asked.

"Another beautiful St. Rob's goal, courtesy of my son," Troy replied with a grin. "Got to take anything we can get. St. Therese is a tough team."

"We've handled them well so far," Marty replied. "Why do I have the feeling Quinn spent most the summer training?"

"Bill Fontana put him through a lot of drills."

"Fontana's still training players? Holy buckets; the guy was around when New Jersey drafted me. What is he now, about seventy?"

"Seventy-two and still one of the toughest trainers I know. Fontana's techniques made Quinn even more disciplined."

"Explains his sharper concentration this year. Maybe I could arrange for Tamar to have a few sessions with Fontana."

"Be warned; he comes with a hefty price tag. I thought you were high on Mike Cabrera working with her and Phil anyway? He's also trained some of the juniors' and AHC's top players."

"Mike's techniques are sublime but Tamar's gotten a little rusty on her goal tending skills from slacking off most of the summer. Both she and Phil need to stay sharp to make college level, juniors or – perhaps a long shot – the pros."

"Don't be an obnoxious hockey dad by pushing them too hard, Marty," Troy said. "I promised Quinn from the time he put on his first pair of skates that I'd support any decision he made. Al and I also encourage him to live much a normal life as possible."

"Shooting pucks in your basement, spending hours at ice rinks, and rarely dating are your ideas of your kid living a 'normal' life?"

"No, but Quinn enjoys practicing on his own. Al and I are okay with him doing so long as his studies aren't affected and he takes breaks to spend time with friends."

"Come to think of it, Tamar could do much worse than stay out past curfew and not practice her goal tending enough. At least she isn't screwing every deadbeat guy in the city, drinking, doing drugs, or failing classes. Would be nice if she and Quinn became an item. He'd make a good son-in-law."

"I doubt they're are considering marrying *anyone* right now, much less each other."

"A father can dream."

"I honestly think Quinn will seek someone more like his mother or Harper after all the drama at his junior prom."

"Ahhh, Harper. Love of my life and best thing that ever happened to me."

Troy grinned. "Better than winning a Princeton Trophy?"

"Never thought I'd say it, but yes. I'd probably never met her if then-Mayor Bisson hadn't invited his staff and a bunch of guys from the Pacific to one of his legendary football-watching gatherings."

"I hope Quinn's as lucky to meet someone who loves him as a *person* and not for social and financial benefits."

Marty patted Troy's shoulder. "Finding women like Harper and Alex are rare in our world. Let me speak from personal experience that Quinn will thank his lucky stars each day when the perfect girl walks into his life. Who knows; it may happen sooner than he, you, and Alex think."

***

PART TWO

April

"Being deeply loved by someone gives you strength, while loving someone deeply gives you courage."

- Lao Tzu

Chapter 20

There are strange synchronicities in which parallel lives gravitate toward one another, shift directions, and then again come close until connections are finally made. Synchronicity can sometimes be tragic – as in repeat of a harrowing experience – while starkly joyful in other situations.

April Stephens entered St. Rob's on scholarship for her junior year of high school. Dr. Mark Stephens and his wife Christine were disillusioned with the public school system's gradual decline; funding cuts, increased violence, drug use, teen pregnancies, and overcrowded classrooms facilitated by teachers that all but gave up making impacts on their students.

As result of such instabilities, many seniors graduated ill-prepared for expectations of the college and employment worlds awaiting them – if some completed high school at all.

April's parents knew her chances of receiving a quality public school education were virtually nil, yet exploring other options was – for most part – out of their reach.

Mark ran a small pediatric medical practice and Christine worked part time at the Clinique counter at Macy's between jobs as a theatrical makeup artist. Despite Mark's bustling patient load and increased demands by several stage productions for Christine's talents, they couldn't afford the soaring tuition costs for private school and their busy schedules made homeschooling April out of the question.

Christine then learned from a theatrical producer about St. Rob's offering scholarships for its upcoming school year. She relayed the information to Mark, cautiously warning him not to tell their daughter in case St. Rob's turned them down despite April being an honor student and participating in activities at her present school.

In the interim, St. Rob's received glowing reports detailing April's grades, her tutoring fellow students, occasionally appearing in small roles or a member of background choral groups in city theater productions, two stints as an extra in Pittsburgh-based films, stellar photography skills, and working at Mark's practice during extended office hours when his front desk help was shorthanded.

The committee concluded that April Christine Stephens would be a perfect addition to St. Rob's student body and offered her a scholarship with alacrity.

While multi-talented with a strong work ethic, April had early difficulties adjusting to her new academic environment. She felt insecure, like a shadow child lurking outside cloistered groups of wealthier, outgoing, and – least by outward appearances – more confident students, never privy to secrets shared by inner circle members.

She viewed herself as unattractive at five feet one inch tall and 157 pounds, but was actually quite pretty with clouds of dark hair tumbling over her shoulders, arresting emerald eyes, porcelain skin, and an engaging smile that displayed perfect teeth.

April found her niche at St. Rob's after securing a spot in its choir. Her strong voice, past musical experience, and wide vocal range captured director Gabriel Legrand's attention. He offered April one of three soloist spots in the choir's Homecoming Week concert.

She couldn't believe her ears. "You think I'm that good?"

"I wouldn't have otherwise selected you, Miss Stephens."

"I know I can sing, but..." April gestured at her body, "always concluded casting people think I'm too fat for solos and lead parts."

Legrand's hand rested under his chin. "I choose students based on *performing* abilities rather than appearance. You're one of my best singers and not having you do a solo would be an abomination on my part. Rehearsals start Friday after school. I look forward to seeing you."

"Thank you, sir. I won't disappoint you."

"You have a bright future in St. Rob's choral program, Miss Stephens. I suggest you take advantage of any and all opportunities offered. Homecoming is only the beginning of many great things you'll experience."

***

Chapter 21

April made her first friend at St. Rob's during choir rehearsals. She'd been preparing to leave after the latest rehearsal when a petite girl with pixie-styled brown hair cheerfully greeted her.

April jumped, startled. "Oh...hi."

"Sorry to scare you. I wanted to say that I love your solo song."

"Thanks; it's from one of my favorite Broadway musicals."

"You're new, right? I never saw you before and the only class we have together is World History."

April nodded. "I won a scholarship to attend St. Rob's this year. My other classes are in Advanced Placement."

"Oooh, a smart girl! You should ace the exam that dick Mr. Oswald is giving us Tuesday. Always nice to see some new faces that aren't among the snobby kids. I'm Lesley St. Cloud."

"April Stephens. St. Cloud? The name sounds familiar."

"Trevor's my older brother and on the boys' hockey team. Our dad played for the Pittsburgh Rebels like a hundred years ago."

"Davy St. Cloud? He coached Team USA in the last Winter Olympics! They won a silver medal."

"You follow hockey?" Lesley asked, surprised.

"Yeah, my father drew me into it. He's watched AHC hockey for years and always follows the Winter Olympics."

"We already have a couple things in common! You have an amazing singing voice. Do you take lessons?"

April chuckled. "I get asked all the time. No, I never had any."

"Naturally talented and brilliant. Some of us should be as lucky."

"You're in choir so you must have *some* talent."

"My parents insisted I participate in extracurricular activities, so I tried out for flag girls and choir. Imagine my surprise when I got picked for both."

"I had the same reaction when Mr. Legrand offered me a solo spot."

"Easy to understand why he did after I heard you sing."

"Are you serious? I'm a whale in comparison to the other two girls he chose."

"You don't look *that* bad. Mr. Legrand's one of a small number of people with ability to spot actual talent." Lesley leaned closer and lowered her voice. "I heard he also has a thing for curvy girls."

"Stop!" April replied with a giggle.

"Nothing wrong with guys liking certain types."

"Ew! He must be at least thirty-five. No offense, but I prefer boys my own age even if none are eager to date me."

"You're new; I'm sure you'll hook up with someone."

"I'm not looking for a 'hook-up'."

"Sorry, bad choice of words. I meant you'll meet some cool guys as the school term progresses."

"We'll see. I know a lot of people tend to think fat girls can't afford to be fussy, but I'd rather go through life single than be jerked around by players."

"I'm sure a guy exists who shares your sentiments. We've barely met, but I can tell you'd make someone a great girlfriend."

"Thanks," April replied with a shy smile.

"What are you doing later? Maybe you'd like to hang out with me and my friend Tamar since she's no longer grounded."

"Sure. Let me call my parents first."

"I would've liked you to meet another friend of ours, but he has practice today."

"Who?"

Lesley grinned. "Quinn Talmadge, captain of the boys' hockey team."

***

Chapter 22

April's initial encounters with Quinn were uneventful; they shared several AP classes and were members of the photography club, yet didn't actually speak to each other early in the school term aside from an occasional "Hi" or "How are you?" He gave her the impression of being a nice guy, but April never imagined being part of his circle – least not at first.

Quinn was Lesley and Tamar's favorite topic. They enjoyed gossiping with April about some of his eccentricities and superstitions: eating peanut butter and jelly sandwiches with the crusts removed each day no matter how close to dinner, personally sharpening the blades of his skates, taping his own sticks (going far as ripping off tape if someone else already done so and re-taping them); avoiding black cats and heights much as possible, not dating on nights before games, wearing the same athletic jock strap since eighth grade (despite comments from teammates and equipment managers about how gross it looked), and how he perfectly lined up a substantial collection of baseball caps on one of his bedroom shelves.

"Quinn tends to be neurotic about certain things," Lesley said, "but it's part of his charm."

"A girl would need lots of patience to deal with his strange rituals," Tamar replied.

"Quinn makes efforts to like everyone, but is all business at the hockey rink, whether it's practicing or actual games."

"He seems nice, at least the few times we came in contact," April said.

Tamar's eyebrows shot up in surprise. "You've already met?"

"Not technically. He's in some of my AP classes, we've said 'hi' to each other, and he's borrowed my notes a few times."

"Well damn, you should try striking up a real conversation."

"Oh no, no, no," April replied in protest. "Quinn Talmadge is *way* out of my league."

"Says who?" Lesley asked. "He likes all kinds of girls."

"Let him know you're a friend of ours," Tamar added. "That should break the ice."

April shook her head. "Maybe I'll wait until he approaches me another time. Is not taking many notes in class another one of his quirks?"

"Quinn's mind is always elsewhere during hockey season," Lesley replied. "He tends to focus more on practices and games than concerning himself with taking immaculate class notes. Maybe slacking on notes is his way of approaching girls he likes, who knows?"

"Hey, you could be on to something, Les," Tamar said. "Phil and I rarely see Quinn study, yet he makes straight A's. Some of us should have such luck. Dad threw a bitch fit and grounded me for two weeks after I got a C on my last math exam, which was funny because math wasn't his best subject either."

"Your dad's always grounding you."

"Yeah, when he's not embarrassing the shit out of me."

"Don't you need to maintain a certain overall grade average to stay on the girls' hockey team, Tamar?" April asked.

"Yeah, but one would think the world ended from hearing Dad's long-winded rant. Geez, it's not like I'm flunking math or any other subject."

"Anyway, more about Quinn," Lesley said. "Did you know Tamar is often his 'default' date?"

"What's that?" April asked. "Sorry, I'm not familiar with some of your lingo."

Tamar gave her an amused grin. "She means I'm Quinn's plus one when he's between girlfriends, which has happened more often recently."

"You've never gone out romantically?"

"Nah. He may be sweet, a total cutie, and the ideal future husband in my father's eyes, but Quinn has too many weird habits for me to tolerate long term. He also tends to be nervous around girls, much as he likes them. Things never worked out with the few he dated."

A quizzical look crossed April's face. "Why would they make him uneasy?"

"You tell us. Maybe the same reason guys scare you."

April gasped. "What gave you that impression?"

"We've seen you get 'deer in headlights' looks when any are present," Lesley replied. "Look how many chances you've had to engage Quinn in longer conversations yet never took advantage."

"Doesn't mean I'm scared of guys. Let's get real; I'm not exactly their ideal type."

"How will you know if you don't make efforts?"

"Believe me, I tried once and that was one time too many."

"What do you mean?" Tamar asked.

April emitted a deep sigh. "One boy approached me about a week after I came to St. Rob's and we started talking. He seemed okay, so I went out with him after school for coffee. We started spending time together before he invited me to a party. I went because I thought it would be perfect for meeting people since my parents nagged me to make new friends. Well...oh God, how can I put this? The party turned out to be a cruel 'pig party' joke with $100 awarded to the guy with the ugliest date! He didn't win the money, but I never felt more humiliated in my life."

"Oh my God, what an asshole! Not to be nosy, but who did that to you?"

"Josh Preston."

"Figures," Lesley said. "He's the basketball team's biggest jerk. Too bad you didn't know us yet; we'd given you advance warnings. You aren't the first transfer girl he pranked and probably not the last."

"Something about Josh gets on my nerves," Tamar replied. "My brother can't stand him either, which is ironic since most of Phil's friends – save Quinn and a few other guys – are jagoffs. I always wanted to punch Josh in the throat."

"Me too, Tams, even if it meant our dads grounding us for a year. I hate Josh with the heat of ten thousand suns."

"Now you know why I'm not eager to date," April said. "Especially jocks, not that I'd have a chance with another one anyway."

"Not all boys are like Josh, April," Lesley assured her. "There *are* decent ones at St. Rob's. Tams and I can say with confidence that Quinn never participated in pig parties or other juvenile crap."

"You're passing on a great opportunity if Quinn's always asking you for notes when he can get them from practically anyone," Tamar said. "Who knows; he may like you more than anyone knows."

"Quit kidding yourselves," April replied. "Let's get back to studying."

***

Chapter 23

Homecoming Week excited and unnerved April. Final choir rehearsals kept her busy, but she found time to cheer on Tamar when the girls' hockey team shut out Our Lady of Mercy's with a 5-0 score and witness the boys defeat St. Arthur's 3-2 after Quinn scored the winning goal.

April sang her solo flawlessly at the choir concert despite feeling uneasy the entire week about how she would be received by the student body and others in attendance. She drew overwhelming amounts of positive feedback to her pleasant surprise, prompting Gabriel Legrand to offer another solo spot for December's holiday concert.

She expected Lesley, Tamar, and her parents' presences in the audience but shocked to see Quinn, Phil, Trevor, and a few other friends seated behind the girls. April was aware boys sometimes "clowned" choir members and soloists during concerts, but no such incidents took place that night.

"Of course they were gentlemen," Lesley said when April later commented on the boys' behavior. "All our parents would otherwise give them the business for acting like assholes in public."

"Quinn doesn't clown choir kids and probably smacked sense into the other guys if they *thought* about doing it," Tamar replied. "By the way, he loved your solo. His words, not mine."

Lesley giggled. "He blushed when Tams and I said he should've told you himself."

"Why would he be embarrassed giving someone a compliment?" April wondered.

"Because he's a goober! Quinn can shoot pucks with the utmost confidence during hockey games, but turns shy as a kid in short pants when urged to say more than 'hello' to a girl since Chanel Jameson dumped him."

"He was too good for her anyway," Tamar said, "but I stand by the belief he likes *you,* April."

April looked skeptical. "Don't you think I'm a considerable downgrade from a cheerleader and model?"

"No way," Lesley said. "Chanel is St. Rob's biggest slag. Rumor has it she's cheating on her current boyfriend, who happens to be one of the guys she was screwing behind Quinn's back."

"She threw him away like used Kleenex during junior prom," Tamar spat. "God, that pissed me off. I could never stand the bitch, but what she did to Quinn made me hate her more. I would've kicked her ass if there was no risk of me being expelled."

April's mouth dropped open. "That's awful! No wonder he's hesitant about talking to girls except you two."

"Quinn's parents said it took him almost all summer to get over the breakup. Thank God for his sister announcing her engagement."

"Wait...isn't she eight years old?"

"Not Noémie, silly!" Lesley replied with a chuckle. "Anna. She's Quinn's older half-sister from his mom's first marriage, but he always viewed her as an actual sister. Anna lived with her dad in Prague, played for a team he owns before she retired, returned to the States, and accepted a position with the San Diego Pacific."

"Anna has a long list of achievements from winning Miss Pennsylvania Teen Princess to being one of the Prague Capitals' biggest on-ice stars," Tamar added. "She's the Pacific's current skating coach. Their players and staff love her."

"She sounds like a great person even if a little intimidating," April said.

"Anna's gorgeous and successful, but far from stuck up in spite of everything she's accomplished. Humble like Quinn, only she speaks her mind more often."

"Quinn's going to be best man at her wedding during holiday vacation," Lesley replied. "Anna's getting married in Pittsburgh. We haven't met her fiance, but hear he's a hot-looking Czech with an exciting career."

April sighed dreamily. "We should all be as lucky."

"Quinn's coming to the football game Friday night," Tamar said. "He attends a lot of them since Phil's on the team."

"You'll be there too, right, April?" Lesley asked.

"Well...I...I don't know..."

"Come on! The other flag girls and I could use you in our cheering section when we perform at halftime."

"You never saw Phil on the football field ," Tamar said. "We're playing St. Thomasina. Their boys' hockey team may have won last year's championship, but their football team sucks big time."

"Okay," April replied. "I'll go, but only because you guys will be there. I have to admit I'd love to see Lesley's flag-twirling skills."

Lesley gave April a broad smile. "I promise not to let you down!"

"Remind me to bring my camera. If you guys insist I go to this game, I want to at least take some pictures for photography club and maybe get some in the yearbook too."

**

Chapter 24

April attended St. Rob's football game as promised, photographing the team in action and Lesley performing with her fellow flag girls during the halftime show.

"This is the best homecoming *ever!*" Tamar shrieked with delight when Phil solidified St. Rob's lead with another touchdown early in the third quarter.

"Your brother's a talented athlete," April said after capturing the moment on camera. "Hockey, basketball, and football. Is there anything he doesn't do?"

"Bowling, and only because I beat his ass every time. God forbid a girl one-ups my evil twin in any type of sport."

"Wow, you bowl too?"

"Yep. My last average was 320."

"I think I got a 95 once. I'm mostly a gutter ball champion."

"You're talented in other areas. For starters, you'd never want to hear me sing and my lousy photography skills can only be viewed on my phone. What are you doing after the game?"

"Probably go home and relax rest of the night. Why?"

"Lesley and I are hanging out at Larry's Pizza. Come with us."

"I have a 12:30 curfew on Fridays when I go out, but okay. Dad's on call at the hospital; I'll let Mom know I'm going with you guys."

"Awesome. A lot of St. Rob's kids go to Larry's. Some have asked about you since the choir concert."

"I never thought anyone else noticed me. I'm only a former public school kid here on scholarship."

"So are a bunch of others. You need to get out more since your singing and photography are opening doors."

"I don't want to make a fool of myself."

"Will you stop? Either people like you or they don't. If they do, great; if not, their damn loss."

"Fine. I'll stay a little while."

"Cool, I'll tell Les you're coming. Never know what will happen while you're there."

"You've made your point, Tamar, now chill." April rolled her eyes, chuckled, and resumed photographing homecoming game memories.

***

Chapter 25

Larry's Pizza was packed when the girls arrived. Lesley and Tamar didn't mind; waiting for a table to open meant they could socialize with other students celebrating St. Rob's homecoming game victory.

April's eyes widened when she spotted the crowd. "You two weren't kidding lots of other kids hang out here."

"Let's go say hi to everyone!" Lesley said.

"Isn't it rude to intrude on other people?" April asked.

Tamar gave her a teasing grin. "Don't worry; most don't bite."

Lesley spotted Quinn with other members of the boys' hockey team. "Hey, Tams, look who's sitting in a back booth with our brothers and their dopey friends."

"Holy buckets!" Tamar cried. "I don't believe it. Quinn *never* comes to post-game gatherings."

"I guess he made an exception for Homecoming," Lesley said. "You girls want to drop by their booth?"

"Nah, you know how Phil and Trevor turn into dicks when they hang out with the team."

April let out a relieved sigh. *Thank you, Tamar.*

"I see JoShan and Tiffany from choir!" Lesley tugged April's sleeve. "Let's go say hi."

"Least they're people I already know," April replied. "A few flag girls are sitting with them too."

"Even better!"

"You guys go ahead," Tamar said. "A table finally opened up and I want to grab it before some jagoff does."

Lesley nodded. "Thanks, Tams. We'll be back to order in a few minutes."

"Take your time. Dad's too wasted to ground me if I miss curfew anyway."

Lesley and April jabbered with their fellow choir members and the few flag girls before joining Tamar at the table she held. They placed food orders and gossiped about the football game as kitchen sounds, animated chatter, shouting, laughter, and general adolescent banter filtered through the pizza restaurant.

All activity suddenly ceased when Phil bellowed for assistance. "Help! Talmadge...he's choking! *He's choking!* Somebody come quick!"

As other students froze in fear, April leaped from her table and darted toward Quinn – who was already turning blue – before a waitress had the chance to intervene.

She grabbed Quinn from behind without a second thought and executed the Heimlich maneuver, causing the remnants of a chewed mozzarella stick to dislodge from his throat and fly across the room.

Quinn gasped as he accepted water from the waitress. "Damn! My whole life passed before my eyes."

"Told you not to eat the mozzarella sticks, dumb ass," Phil replied. "You almost choked the last time you had them. I swear sometimes you have a death wish."

Quinn turned his attention to April. "Wow, did I die and go to the pretty girls' section in heaven?"

The question made her blush. "Are you okay?"

He gave her a friendly smile. "I am now."

"Thanks for your help," Trevor said, his voice heavy with gratitude. "God knows what outcome we may have had if you weren't here."

"I'm sure the waitress would've done something," April assured him.

"What thing did you...?" Phil asked.

"The Heimlich. My father taught me how to do it. He's a pediatrician."

"Hey," Quinn said. "You're in some of my AP classes and sang at the homecoming concert."

April nodded. "That's me."

"I bummed notes from you a few times. Your name's like some month. August...May...June...?"

His guessing made her laugh. "April. April Stephens."

"Right, *April.*"

"Are you sure you're okay?"

"Never better, considering I almost lost my life."

"Maybe now you'll listen to me and not eat any more mozzarella sticks," Phil said.

"Chill out, Phil." Quinn's violet eyes remained fixated on April. "You're pretty. I *love* brunettes."

Connor cracked a knowing smile. "Yet the few girls you dated or banged were blondes."

"Shut up, Williams."

"Don't mind Talmadge, April," Jay Gold said. "I think the temporary loss of oxygen made our boy goofy."

"I'm fine, dude." Quinn turned back to April. "What are you doing next weekend?"

She eyed him warily. "Why do you ask?"

"Jay's having a birthday party at his house next Saturday and I don't have anyone to take with me. Would you like to go?"

April balked. "Well...I..."

"Lesley and Tams told me about the mean stunt Josh pulled. I'm better than that loser." Quinn held up his hands. "No pranks. Promise."

Her demeanor softened. "Okay, you have a date."

"Let's exchange numbers in case anything changes or we don't get any chances to talk at school."

She agreed, tapped Quinn's number into her phone's contact list, and gave him hers. "See you Monday."

"Thanks again for saving my life." He gave her a wink. "Literally."

***

Chapter 26

April arrived at school the following Monday bemused about attending Jay's party with Quinn. Despite assuring her he'd never play tricks the way Josh Preston had, April couldn't help but still question Quinn's actual intentions.

"How many times do we have to tell you Quinn's one of the school's classiest guys?" Tamar asked during lunch. "Do you have any idea how many girls would jump at the chance to date him?"

"Not to mention it's been forever since he took out anyone except Tams," Lesley replied.

Tamar broke into a huge grin. "I could use a break, you know. Our brothers are still amazed how you saved Quinn from choking to death. You're a hero."

"Going to the party with Quinn is his way of showing appreciation," Lesley said.

"I only acted on instinct," April replied. "He could've found better ways to thank me than being his 'mercy date'."

"Will you stop beating up yourself all the time?" Tamar asked. "Quinn's a gentleman and mature, unlike some other St. Rob's jocks whose names I won't mention."

"I know Phil and Trevor through you guys, but what are Quinn's other friends actually like? I only talked to them a few minutes Friday night."

"Jay's cool. He likes meeting new people and is also a scholarship kid. Connor's kind of weird and thinks about sex a lot, but otherwise okay. Demond, Hank, Nick, and Logan play a lot of pranks – not mean like Josh's – and won't exactly be mistaken for Rhodes Scholars anytime soon. They're all hilarious and nice, though. By the way, I should warn you that Phil and Trevor tend to act like jagoffs when other guys are present."

"Thanks," April said. "I don't have a lot of experience with boys, so every bit of information helps."

Lesley giggled. "Tams failed to mention you should keep an eye on Carl. He likes girls with 'some flesh on them' and may try to grab or smack your butt."

"Not in Quinn's presence if Carl values his life," Tamar said. "Carl's not the chandelier's brightest bulb, but at least he's cute."

"Then why not go out with him?" April asked.

"Not my type. Dad wouldn't let me date Carl anyway."

"He's still holding out hope of Quinn someday being his son-in-law?" Lesley teasingly asked.

Tamar snorted. "He's a delusional pain in the ass."

"What should I wear?" April wondered.

Lesley stared at her wide-eyed. "Huh?"

"The party I'm going to with Quinn. I bought some nice leggings but haven't had a chance to wear them yet. Will they be okay?"

"The Golds aren't fancy people so don't bother dressing up for Jay's party. Your new leggings and a sweater will look great."

"Keep your hair the same as Friday and today," Tamar added. "Quinn loves it."

April gave her an incredulous look. "How do you know?"

"He may have been with almost every type of girl, but natural-looking ones are his favorites."

Lesley gave April a lighthearted nudge. "One who knows how to do the Heimlich maneuver is even better."

"Stop!" April exclaimed laughingly. "Sorry for all the questions. I'm nervous about the party and don't want to make Quinn look like a loser."

Tamar leaned forward. "Trust me, April, he won't feel any more embarrassed than he did at Larry's Pizza the other night no matter what happens. Relax, be yourself, concentrate on having a good time, and give us all the details afterward."

***

Chapter 27

The next few days passed without incident before April woke Thursday morning with pain in her lower right side, drifting between feeling nauseous, warm, and chilled.

Christine insisted her daughter remain home after noticing her lethargic appearance and feeling her forehead.

"I probably slept on my side wrong and got some dumb bug that will be gone later," April protested. "Give me a couple aspirin so I can get ready for school."

"You'll do no such thing, missy. Your father and I didn't jump through hoops to get you a St. Rob's scholarship so you could infect its entire student body with some godforsaken illness."

"Mom, I-"

"*No,*" Christine sternly replied and called downstairs to her husband. "Mark! Could you bring your thermometer?"

"What's wrong?" he asked.

"April's not feeling well."

"I'll be fine, Mom," she said through clenched teeth.

"You're staying home whether you like it or not," Christine said. "I'll call the dean and let him know you're not coming to school today."

"God, you're dramatic."

"I can bring up some soup after Dad takes your temperature."

"I'm not hungry and want to lose five more pounds before Saturday."

"Why? The boy who asked you to be his date has no problem with how much you weigh."

"Mom, he's captain of the hockey team and doesn't need to show up with someone who looks like Orca."

"Now you're being silly."

"I don't know why I bother talking to you."

Mark appeared in the room with the black bag he often carried to his office. "You should listen to your mother, April."

"You should stop treating me like a child, Dad," she replied before he placed the thermometer into her ear. "I'm not one of your patients."

Mark's eyes widened as he mentally noted April's elevated temperature. He gently pressed around several areas of her lower abdomen.

April jumped and yelped in pain. "Damn! What are you trying to do, kill me?"

"Just as I suspected," he said. "Fever, chills, radiating lower abdominal pain, lethargy. Rest and soup are the last things you need, young lady. You're going to the emergency room *now.*"

***

Chapter 28

Quinn crept into April's hospital room, making efforts to remain quiet as possible. He set a vase of white roses he brought on the bedside table and gazed at her dozing figure from a nearby chair.

April awakened and sensed a presence in the room. "Quinn?"

"Hey. Hi," he said in a soft voice. "How are you feeling?"

"Okay I guess. What are you doing here?"

"Some other kids and I got worried when no one saw you at school since you aren't exactly known for ditching classes. I tried calling, but got no answer. Your mom told Lesley, Tamar and Carl you were in the hospital when they brought your homework assignments."

"How did you know my room number?"

"Your mom gave it to Lesley and the other two in case anyone from school wanted to visit."

"I'm surprised to see you. Excuse me being a mess."

"You're fine; no one in real life looks like they came off a magazine cover with every hair in place after having surgery."

"Thanks. Guess I won't be going to Jay's party after all. Wish there was something I could do to make up inconveniencing you."

"I'd hardly consider your appendectomy an inconvenience. We could always hang out when you feel better."

April brightened. "You mean that?"

"Sure. I was also thinking you could meet my family sometime."

"Maybe in the future after we've spent more time together."

Their exchange was interrupted by April's parents entering the room.

Christine kissed April's cheek. "I'm sorry, honey. We didn't know you had company."

Mark walked over to Quinn and introduced himself. "We're April's parents. I'm Dr. Mark Stephens and this is my wife Christine."

Quinn stood and shook Mark's hand. "Quinn Talmadge. A pleasure, sir."

"Oh, the boy who was going to take April to a party this weekend!" Christine replied. "Glad to finally meet you."

"Wish we had under better circumstances, Mrs. Stephens."

"I'd planned to bring Quinn home with me today after school since he didn't have practice," April said. "Unfortunately, my idea fell through for obvious reasons."

"Practice?" Christine asked him. "Are you also in choir?"

Quinn laughed. "Oh no, ma'am. Singing's your daughter's domain. I can't carry a tune to save my own life."

"Mom!" April cried. "I told you several times Quinn's captain of the boys' hockey team."

Mark raised an eyebrow. "Hockey, huh? I happen to enjoy the sport. I'd ask if you were related to Troy Talmadge, but he's Canadian."

"So am I, sir," Quinn said. "I was also born in Yarmouth, Nova Scotia. Troy's my dad."

"Well I'll be damned. He was one of my favorite players back in the day. Troy, Boris Furishnykov, Jax Ivanka, Davy St. Cloud, Pierre Germaine...all Princeton Trophy legends. If someone said I'd someday sit in the same room as the son of a former AHC superstar, I'd question their sanity. Yet here we are."

"Dad, come on; you're embarrassing Quinn," April interjected. "The overgrown fanboy act does not flatter you."

"No, no, it's okay," Quinn replied. "Discussing hockey with someone besides my teammates and my parents' friends is refreshing." He again addressed Mark. "I asked April if she'd like to meet my parents sometime before you and Mrs. Stephens arrived. Maybe I can extend the invitation for the two of you to join us."

"I'd be honored," Mark said and turned to his wife. "What do you think, Chris?"

"How about April meeting them first?" Christine suggested. "We shouldn't overwhelm the Talmadges."

"Good idea." Mark checked his watch. "I'm on call this evening and need to get downstairs." He gave April a quick kiss on the cheek. "I'll check with Dr. Harris as to when he plans to discharge you. Meanwhile, get some rest and don't give the nurses a hard time."

"I won't, Dad."

"I should also be going," Christine said. "I'm expecting a call from City Theater about possibly doing makeup for their production of *The Wiz*."

"Hope you get the gig, Mom. See you guys tomorrow."

***

Chapter 29

"Sorry about my father," April said after her parents were gone. "I'm surprised you weren't further interrogated after telling him about your dad."

"No apology needed," Quinn replied. "He and your mom are cool people. What kind of medicine does your dad practice?"

"Pediatrics. He has a small office about two blocks from the hospital and on call three nights a week."

"I bet his patients love him."

"Oh, both they and the parents do! Dad has a knack for dealing with fussy and scared kids during their appointments. He told me once he decided on pediatrics after I had colic and ear infections as a baby."

"You were colicky?" Quinn asked, wide-eyed. "Me too! My life got off to a bumpy start; I was born premature and not expected to live."

"Your parents must've been relieved when you beat the odds."

"To say the least," Quinn replied. "I never heard you mention brothers or sisters. Do you have any?"

"I'm an only child. Dad was still an intern when Mom had me. She took a job and was still in school. We moved in with my grandparents; Nana Stephens took care of me while my parents and grandfather worked. Papa Stephens had a podiatry practice."

"Sounds like your early life was unsettling."

"I wouldn't describe it that way at all," April said. "I loved spending time with Nana. She took me to the park, matinee plays, kids' museums, and outdoor concerts. I loved hearing her sing; she did local TV commercial jingles before marrying Papa. Mom says I inherited Nana's talent."

"You are an outstanding singer. Do you plan to follow in your grandmother's footsteps?"

"No, I'd like to become a pediatric nurse or maybe open a day care center." April smiled at him. "I'll bet you'll continue the Talmadge family tradition of playing hockey."

"You already know me well. I'm considering sports medicine if hockey doesn't work out. A couple schools offered me scholarships."

"Have you decided on a college?"

"Not yet."

"Me neither. I'd like to go to one with top-notch nursing or business programs."

"I'm sure you'll have no problem getting into a good school. You got a St. Rob's scholarship and take AP classes, so you're no dummy." Quinn leaned forward in his chair. "Now that we discussed the distant future, let's talk about the near one. What would you like to do after leaving the hospital?"

April chuckled. "Are you asking me for another date?"

"I haven't taken you on a first one yet, so yeah."

"A movie would be nice. Nothing scary, though. I'll have nightmares for weeks afterward."

"I prefer comedies myself, but we can decide on other things to do when you get out."

"Sounds great. I should have some idea when I'm leaving this place after Dr. Harris comes tomorrow."

"Okay for me to drop by after school?" Quinn asked.

"Of course! You don't need to bother asking."

"Then we'll meet again tomorrow afternoon. Get some rest; I want you at full strength when we go on our first date."

***

Chapter 30

April left the hospital five days after her appendectomy. She was eager to resume classes and catch up with friends despite Christine insisting she remain home until the following Monday.

"Dr. Harris said resume activities as tolerated," April said. "I can tolerate school."

"I know, sweetheart, but don't think it's wise to jump back into things after you've had major surgery," Christine replied. "Taking off a few more days won't hurt. Lesley, Tamar, and Carl have been bringing your homework so it's not like you're behind at school."

"I still have to take a few exams."

"Your teachers will understand and arrange make-up dates."

"I'm *bored,* Mom, and miss my friends."

Christine gave her daughter a knowing smile and placed an arm around her shoulder. "I may have an idea why you're gung ho about school. A young man named Quinn Talmadge."

April's cheeks flushed with crimson. *"Mom!"*

"No need to be embarrassed about having a crush, sweetheart. I was once sixteen too."

"I'm not crushing on Quinn. He visited me in the hospital and we're going out next weekend. I don't know where we're going and he won't tell me."

"He's such a nice young man. All boys should be as gallant and polite."

"Quinn is also out of my league. I don't know why he bothers with me aside from us being in photography club and a few classes together."

"I wish you weren't so hard on yourself. You're beautiful, kind, intelligent, and talented; the ideal young woman for any man with half a brain. Why wouldn't Quinn want to take you out?"

"Because I'm better suited as a Sea World attraction than his date?"

"Don't be ridiculous, April. I never wore a size two either but that didn't bother your father when we dated."

"Dad doesn't strike me as the shallow type anyway."

"He never was, and I received the same vibes from Quinn. I'm sure he'd also want you to stay home from school a few more days to save your strength for the big date."

"Okay, but at least let me have friends over to help study for my make-up exams."

"They're welcome to visit any time long as your father isn't on call overnight. He needs his rest."

"No problem."

"We're delighted seeing you have friends among the decent kids. I also think Carl has a crush on you. Quinn better stay sharp if he's going to keep any competition at bay."

"There's no competition for me, Mom. Carl's a good friend but too flighty for possible dating material. Besides, I like dark-haired boys."

"Like your father," Christine said.

"Yeah; too bad I have yet to meet any guys with a personality similar to his. Most my age have one thing on their minds."

"I only met Quinn a few times, but don't get the impression he's among those kinds of boys, April."

"I hope you're right, Mom. I thought Josh was nice too and we both know how he turned out."

"Perhaps you can view that experience as dodging a bullet. Think about it; if you'd continued wasting your time chasing Josh after he pulled that awful stunt, you'd never been at the pizza parlor with your friends and saved Quinn from choking. The perfect story to tell your children someday."

"Mom! We haven't gone on a date yet and you're bringing up the idea of *grandchildren?*"

"I'm sure the same thing has crossed his parents' minds at least once."

"Quinn's headed to college next year and focused on hockey. I doubt he's thought about having kids, and who's to say we'll get married?"

"Anything is possible, honey."

"Calm down, Mom." She gave Christine a teasing grin. "Some people never have the opportunity to marry a brilliant medical intern turned pediatrician."

"You did something right to catch the eye of a prominent sports family's handsome scion, young lady."

"Now let's hope this possible prince doesn't turn out to be another frog like Josh Preston."

"Quinn won't," Christine replied. "I'll bet the mortgage on it."

***

PART THREE

Love and Hockey

"Give me some sugar, baby."

- Paul Martin

Chapter 31

"Hey, April!" Quinn cheerfully greeted her Monday morning. "Welcome back!"

She gasped, startled. "Quinn...hi."

He leaned against a locker with hands stuffed in his pockets. "Feeling okay?"

"Much better and glad to be back in school. My parents drove me crazy after I came home from the hospital."

"Glad to hear it. I can't wait for Saturday night."

"Does this mean you'll finally tell me where we're going?" April asked.

"What, and spoil the surprise? No way."

"Lesley and Tamar were right; you *are* a total goober."

"They were also spot on that you're a pretty and sweet girl."

April felt her knees weaken and braced the locker for support. Quinn reached behind, removed her backpack, and slung it across his shoulder. She noticed other students staring at their exchange, likely wondering why Quinn was chatting with her. He usually hung with other boys, rarely speaking to girls in great lengths – except Lesley and Tamar – unless necessary.

"You don't have to do that," she said, closing her locker.

"I don't mind. Think of it as a workout for me."

April nervously giggled. "As if you need another workout."

They walked down the corridor talking and laughing. A group of football players darted toward them, tossing a football at one another. One boy caught it and plowed into April at breakneck speed. She yelped, staggered backward, and lost her balance.

Quinn quickly grabbed April and pulled her close with a firm grip as she placed her hands on his shoulders. She looked up and noticed their faces were inches apart.

"Are you okay?" he asked with genuine concern.

"Yeah....thanks for the quick save."

Quinn set April upright, motioned for her to wait, and then walked toward the group of football players. "Hey, dope fucks, watch where the hell you're going next time you tear ass down the hall! You almost knocked down this poor girl."

April's mouth dropped open, taken aback by his sudden hostile demeanor.

Quinn sized up the group of guys, their larger sizes not intimidating him. "She had her appendix out last week could've been seriously hurt."

"Geez, sorry, Talmadge," one replied.

"Don't tell *me*. Say it to April or I'll give you all reasons to be sorry."

The boys apologized and then went their separate ways. April ducked her head, uncomfortable with the attention, while Quinn walked her to their class.

"Was any of that necessary?" she asked. "I already said I'm okay. Save your aggression for hockey games."

"Those morons needed taught a lesson. You should understand up front that when people I care about are hurt, I defend them to the death." Quinn gave her a reassuring smile. "You could say it's another quirk I possess as both team captain and having two sisters."

"Oh...I'll keep that in mind."

"I have to leave for an appointment after class, but may I catch up with you later?"

"Of course; I'll take notes in classes you miss and make copies."

"Thanks, I appreciate the help."

April sneaked glimpses of Quinn throughout class, wondering if he'd been a lonely child or outcast because of his family name, ultra focus on hockey, skill set, and envied by less popular boys despite the large groups of people drawn to him. She wanted to know more of the *real* Quinn Talmadge aside from Lesley and Tamar's glossed over details, and hoped their Saturday night date would be a perfect opportunity.

***

Chapter 32

April joined Lesley and Tamar at their usual lunch table. Carl Sundersson plopped next to them and plucked a couple French fries from Tamar's tray.

She smacked his hand, annoyed.

"Ow!" Carl exclaimed. "Shit, Tammy, what's wrong with you?"

"Get your own food and stop calling me Tammy."

"Okay, okay. No need to get an attitude."

"Try taking stuff from my tray again and you'll be lucky to get those fingers back."

"You gingers have no souls."

"I'll be happy to steal yours while you sleep."

April barely hid an amused grin. "How's your day so far, Carl?"

"I wish we had longer weekends. Coach brought us in for extra practice all day Saturday and then my dad took me to a Rebels game yesterday afternoon for some 'father-son time.' Things heating up with you and Talmadge, huh? People are talking about how he practically camped at the hospital after you had your appendix out and was ready to beat the shit out of some dude for nearly knocking you on your ass."

April choked on her beverage. "Where did you hear that?"

"From some guys on the hockey team and a few of their girlfriends."

"Oh my God!" Lesley cried. "Is that true, April?"

"Well, everything except Quinn 'camping' at the hospital. He visited a grand total of three times. Geez, news travels fast in this school."

"Did you expect anything different? Girls love him and boys want to be him. He's the ideal guy."

"Yet humble, charming, mature, and sweet, just like you told me."

"I'll be happy to let Quinn know," a voice behind them said.

April turned and faced a grinning Phil, who extended a hand to high-five Carl.

Tamar glared at him. "What the hell's your problem? Did you get exiled from your table or something?"

"I can't say hello to my little sister and her friends?" Phil asked.

"May I remind you once more we're only seven minutes apart? You and Dad are like diapers; always on my ass and full of shit."

"For someone who thinks the old man's a pain, you have more of his personality traits than I do."

"Yeah, but both your faces can break mirrors and scare children."

April derailed the litany of playful insults. "I'm sure you didn't come by to heckle Tamar."

"I talked to Quinn ten minutes ago," Phil replied. "He said you'd have notes from classes he missed."

"Oh yeah!" She opened her backpack and handed him a folder. "Everything he needs is in here."

"Thanks; I'll give this to him at practice." Phil wiggled his eyebrows. "Your date will be interesting, to say the least."

April's eyes widened. "You know where we're going?"

"I have a general idea."

"Ugh! He can tell his friends but not much as give *me* a hint? Quinn Talmadge is going to be in a world of trouble tomorrow."

"You can yell at him before then. He wants you to come and watch practice."

"Seriously?"

"Yeah. Hockey team practices are open to students Mondays and Tuesdays."

"Well, I planned to study with the girls and-"

"Go, April," Lesley encouraged her. "We can have study group anytime."

"Here's your chance to watch Quinn whoop my evil twin's fat ass around the ice," Tamar replied.

"You ain't shit, Tam-Tam," Phil retorted.

"By the way, you owe Dad forty-seven bucks for gas. He said there was barely half an inch left in the tank after you last used his car."

"Shit, almost half of this week's allowance already blown."

"Maybe next time you'll remember to stop at a gas station, you dick." Tamar glanced at April. "Be grateful you don't have any siblings."

"I miss having a brother or sister sometimes," April replied. "Being an only child isn't always what it's cracked up to be."

"You can make up for it by having a family with Quinn someday," Phil teased her.

"Goodbye, Phil," Tamar said, "and take Carl's fry thieving ass with you."

Carl rose from his seat. "I see Jay and Hank. Catch you at practice, April."

"Bye. Say hi to the other guys for me."

Tamar addressed April when the boys were gone. "Quinn honestly didn't say where he's taking you Saturday night?"

"Not a word. Looks like Phil's staying quiet too."

"Which is rare; my brother usually can't keep a secret to save his own life."

"I could torture Trevor until he gives me a hint," Lesley offered. "Wait! Maybe you're meeting Quinn's parents."

April shook her head. "No, I'm sure he would've given me advance warning if that was the case."

"True; Chanel didn't meet them until after she went out with Quinn three or four times."

"Do you guys have other ideas?"

"No, but it must be something special for him to make efforts to keep everything under wraps," Tamar said. "Quinn didn't say anything to Les and me either because he was afraid we'd leak details."

"He's right," Lesley replied. "We would've never kept such a thing from you."

"I suppose I can wait until Saturday. What's the worst that can happen?" April asked.

"That's the spirit!" Lesley said. "All you need to do is enjoy yourself and let everything fall into place."

Tamar nodded in agreement. "Whatever Quinn has planned, we're confident he'll make sure it's an evening both of you will remember the rest of your lives. The only other thing we ask is a report next Monday."

April tittered. "You girls will be first to know all the details."

***

Chapter 33

Quinn took April to an ice rink Saturday night following dinner. She inwardly panicked, hesitant to inform him of her lacking skating experience as he bolted towards the ice.

He offered an outstretched hand. "Grab my hand and come on the ice. You're about to have the time of your life!"

"What gave you the insane idea to bring me ice skating on our first date? I've never-"

"Didn't you tell me not long ago that you wanted to try new things? Come on; it will be fun."

"What if I fall?"

"I'll catch you. Promise."

"You better have a good explanation prepared for my parents if I get any bruises or broken bones."

"Not going to happen on my shift. Come on; it will be fun."

"You've completely lost your mind."

"I'm right here to catch you."

Quinn held back a colossal grin as she gripped his hands for dear life. He slowly skated backwards, facing April as she remained in a rigid stance to keep her balance, sensing she'd held her breath since stepping foot onto the ice.

She opened her eyes and exhaled after Quinn squeezed her hands in a reassuring manner. He pulled her for several moments, watching as April slowly placed one foot in front of the other, gradually increasing her strides with newfound confidence.

"Oh my God, Quinn!" she cried with joy. "I'm skating!"

"You're doing great. Now aren't you glad you tried?"

"Yes!" April slid her hands from Quinn's for a moment. "Let me do a little more."

He gave her an encouraging smile. "Don't let me stop you."

April attempted skating unassisted for a few moments, quickly lost her balance, and pitched backward with a loud yip. Quinn caught her in remarkable haste and helped hold her upright as she kept slipping, his firm hold preventing her from falling.

Quinn stood behind her and rested his hands on her hips. He gently pushed forward, found April's hands placed above his, and intertwined his fingers with hers.

"Do you feel comfortable going a little faster?" he asked before slightly picking up the pace.

"Sure, why not?"

He took off, pushing April in front of him at a soaring speed, relishing the moment while she laughed and squealed, her arms spread like angel wings. He delighted in watching her newfound confidence bloom and wanted to hold on to the moment long as possible.

April managed to turn and face him skating backward, an attentive smile on her face. "What?"

"Nothing..."

"Come on, Quinn; you're not fooling me. Speak your mind."

"I can't help but think how much you're changing since we got together," he replied.

"Together? We mostly hung out at school and a couple of your hockey practices before tonight."

"Yeah, but now you attend more events, talk to people besides Lesley and Tamar, and appear more comfortable than you did beginning of school year."

"You *noticed* all that?"

"I have a confession, April. I've watched you since the first day you walked into AP Chemistry."

His sudden revelation caught her off guard. "Why didn't you...?"

"I was afraid of looking like a desperate jerk." Quinn lowered his head and shoved his hands in his pockets. "I, uh, asked Lesley and Tamar who you were and if you had a boyfriend."

April broke out in a hearty laugh. "Quinn Talmadge, you little sneak! You're a fine person to talk about someone being awkward around the opposite sex."

He cleared his throat. "I haven't had much luck with girls, contrary to popular belief."

"I know," she softly replied. "The girls filled me in about you."

"I should've guessed," Quinn said with a chuckle. "Both have big mouths, especially Tams."

"You're the sweetest guy I've ever met and can't understand why anyone would treat you bad."

He shrugged. "Guess not many girls want my type anymore."

"Well it's their damn loss!"

Quinn pecked her cheek. "You're cute."

April's face flushed. "Thanks...I think. Are you going to teach me to ice skate some more?"

"Ready whenever you are, but I want to ask one more thing."

"What?"

"How would you like to meet my family next weekend?"

"Shouldn't we go out a couple more times before making such a big leap?"

"I'd agree if it you were anyone else, but my parents have been nagging me to bring you home since I told them about the choking incident at Larry's Pizza. My older sister's making a rare visit from San Diego and also wants to meet you."

Quinn's offer intrigued April. "Okay, let me know what day next weekend. Meanwhile, I'd like to resume our skating lesson unless you have something else in mind."

He clasped her hands. "No, I have all I need right here."

***

Chapter 34

"Wow!" Tamar gasped when April relayed Quinn's offer at school the following Monday. "You're definitely special if he's moving that fast. Quinn usually waits a certain period of time before bringing home girls. Well, at least the rare times he does."

"I'm a little nervous," April said.

"Don't be; you'll love his parents and Noémie's a little cutie," Lesley replied.

"Quinn told me his older sister will be in town."

Lesley nodded. "Anna emailed me and Tams. The Pacific gave her a few days off. She's coming to take care of last-minute wedding stuff."

"She told us Quinn talked about you all the time during their Skype sessions," Tamar said with a humongous grin.

April let out a low groan. "By the way, I don't recall either of you mentioning you discussed me with him not long after school started."

"Where did you...?"

"He told me Saturday night."

"Quinn kept pestering us," Lesley said. "He'd been checking you out on the sly during classes, so Tams and I told him what little we knew at the time."

"Now you know why we encouraged you to date him," Tamar replied.

April shook her head, amused. "I should've suspected something when he always asked to copy my class notes."

"Be flattered. Quinn didn't talk to as many people about Chanel or other ex-girlfriends."

"He barely discussed them with us or our brothers outside school," Lesley added.

"I don't consider myself his girlfriend," April protested, "at least not yet in the traditional sense."

"Quinn wouldn't suggest meeting his family so soon if you didn't mean *something* to him. A true relationship involves more than tonsil tickling, holding hands, other kinds of showing affection, or sending each other mushy texts."

"I can't recall the last time something besides hockey made him this happy," Lesley said. "You succeeded doing what no other girl could, April – breaking through his invisible wall."

***

Chapter 35

"I hope I'm not moving too fast," Quinn said to a few teammates before hockey practice. "I invited April to meet Mom and Dad this coming weekend."

"Sounds like things are getting serious," Jay Gold replied. "Good for you, man."

"I'm afraid of fucking up things with her the way I did Chanel."

"Dude," Hank Geary spoke up. "There are wide differences between a nice girl like April and Cum Dumpster Chanel. Rest assured you'll have a difficult time pissing off April short of committing some type of unpardonable sin."

"Geary's right," Demond Brown replied. "April doesn't unravel over the smallest things. Cum Dumpster Chanel's fine, but she's a petty bitch."

Connor guffawed. "Good for quick blow jobs in the school john or back seat booty calls, though."

"God damn, Williams, are there girls at this school you *haven't* fucked?" Trevor asked, grimacing.

"Your sister, O'Freel's twin, and April. Not only none of them my type, but I also don't want to risk being murdered by you, O'Freel, and the Cap."

"Tam-Tam could easily kick your ass herself," Phil joked. "I'm not the only one Dad taught how to fight like a man on *and* off the ice."

A dreamy look crossed Carl's face. "Hey Talmadge, if you ever get tired of April, remember to send her my way."

Phil gave him an annoyed look. "You're not helping, Sundersson."

"Damn right he isn't. Everybody in this room is fucking dead if they much as look at April in ways I don't like," Quinn said.

"Wow, Cap, I am liking this side of you," Connor replied. "First you wanted to fuck up some asshole on the football team, now you're preparing to hit kill mode if anyone tries to steal your girl."

"What did I tell you dumb shits?" Trevor asked. "April's been a good influence on the man."

Quinn basked in how well his teammates accepted April. "You're all exaggerating, but thanks."

Logan Burns clapped his shoulder. "Anytime, bro. I could identify with April being on the outside looking in before I met Jeni. Who thought a guy like me from hick ass Washington County would get with one of St. Rob's hottest cheerleaders?" He winked. "All her bendy moves aren't limited to pep rallies and games either."

"Too much information, Burns." Quinn turned to the others. "So you guys don't think it's too soon for April to meet my parents?"

"Are you kidding?" Phil asked. "They've been on your ass for God knows how long."

"Plus she's cute, smart, and doesn't open her legs for anything with a dick," Jay replied. "What's the problem?"

Quinn drew out a long sigh. "I'm worried about Mom picking apart April. She's hated every girl I brought home."

"Don't be so sure, man," Phil said. "I have a feeling Alex is looking forward to finally meeting the one person responsible for saving her baby boy from a horrible death."

"April could charm Satan," Trevor assured Quinn. "Everything will be fine, man."

Quinn rose from the bench and grabbed his hockey sticks. "I suppose I'll know for sure this weekend. We better get to the ice before Coach opens a vein wondering where we are."

***

Chapter 36

While she and Troy encouraged Quinn to bring April home for dinner, Alex Talmadge remained doubtful that the girl would live up to her son's enthusiastic description.

Past girlfriends had taken advantage of Quinn's kind and generous nature, only to be cast aside when they grew tired of him or he no longer served their social-climbing purposes. Alex assumed April was no different and prepared accordingly to deal with her.

"You should keep more of an open mind, Al," Troy advised her.

"Quinn's been hurt too many times by scholarship girls," Alex replied. "I know we've wanted to meet April for some time, but I'm still skeptical about her."

"You always find something negative about every girl. We're discussing someone who prevented Quinn from choking to death during homecoming weekend. Name *one* of his exes who would've done the same. I'll wait."

"Yes, April may have saved his life, but how do you know she doesn't have an agenda of her own?"

"For starters, she's an high honor student, choir soloist, photography club secretary, scored a 1530 on the SAT's, hangs out with Tamar and Lesley, and shares several AP classes with Quinn. Her father's a doctor – far from filthy rich but has a stellar reputation – and her mother's done makeup for several theater productions. The girl can't get more upstanding."

"You thought Chanel was upstanding too."

"Which is why I conducted further research on April and her family. What I found further convinced me that Quinn finally found a decent girl. Do you honestly believe St. Rob's outstanding hockey season is the sole reason for his recent giddy mood?"

"Hmmm...I have noticed him behaving different than usual," Alex replied.

Troy smirked. "Promise you'll refrain from over-analyzing every little thing about April and interrogating her."

"Okay, but that depends on whether or not I pick up bad vibes."

"You're impossible."

"I don't relish the thought of Quinn's career goals and reputation suffering as a result of him besotted with some girl. Do you remember what happened to Lenny Walton after he got arrested with a stripper for cocaine possession?"

"He and Quinn are different people, Al. I've seen players like Lenny lured by the AHC's perks of fame, big money, lucrative endorsement contracts, shots at representing their native countries in the Olympics, and having parades of women – or in some cases, *men* – at their feet. Those same players seldom took their careers seriously and ended up either traded to the minors for younger and hungrier prospects, reduced to playing in near-obscure leagues overseas, or went totally bankrupt. Quinn would still put his hockey aspirations first whether he's dating the world's hottest supermodel, a major corporation's CEO, or an everyday girl next door."

Alex gave a resigned sigh. "Fine, you made your point, but I swear to God if -"

"I know I'm right this time. You should consider hearing my input more often before jumping to conclusions."

"Don't get cocky, mister. Now I need to check on dinner before Quinn and April get here."

"Everything smells terrific," Troy said. "Making your famous spaghetti?"

"Yes, I'm using the sauce recipe everyone loves," Alex replied. "Anna is also due soon. Could you watch for her since I haven't had time to activate the motion sensor lights yet? Lord knows we don't need Marty standing at the end of our driveway a second time with his rifle pressed against Anna's driver's side window because he didn't recognize her rental car."

Troy rose from his chair. "No problem. I'll switch on the motion sensors and keep an eye out for Quinn too."

***

Chapter 37

Aromas of tomato sauce and garlic drew Quinn to the kitchen, where he was caught off guard seeing his mother instead of their housekeeper prepare dinner.

Alex turned and smiled. "Hi, honey! Bet you never guessed someone with Scottish blood could make the right kind of spaghetti sauce *not* from a can."

"I didn't expect you to cook at all," Quinn said. "Where's Francine?"

"I gave her the weekend off since Anna's in town and you were bringing April for dinner." Alex glanced behind him. "Where are you hiding her?"

"She's getting something from the car. Mom, not to be mean, but co-owning the Rebels far outweighs your culinary skills, hence one reason Dad hired Francine. Trying to impress April by making dinner isn't one of your best ideas."

Alex held out a spoon. "Some young man apparently forgot my knack for making spaghetti."

Quinn tasted the offered sample, pleasantly surprised by the bouquet of flavors on his tongue. "Wow, what did you do different? This is better than I remember!"

"Harper gave me a recipe her late father used in his restaurant after I grew tired of using canned sauce and your dad complained my homemade was too spicy. Spaghetti night is the only time he *won't* let Francine in the kitchen."

"I take back what I said earlier about you lacking kitchen skills."

"Francine still does most of the cooking, so don't get comfortable with me slaving over a stove. She made her homemade bread dough before leaving for the weekend, and I have a loaf in the oven as we speak. The rest of us would like to have at least one slice before you and your father devour the whole thing."

"I'll definitely save some for April. Francine's bread is the best."

"Could you get Noémie from the horse barn? Everything's almost ready and Anna should be coming any minute."

"Sure, Mom. I'll be back in a few."

A car horn diverted Alex's attention. "There's Anna now. She'll probably need help with her luggage."

"No problem," Quinn replied. "Pickle and I can give her a hand. Mom, could you also make an effort to…?"

Alex nodded and gave him a knowing smile. "Don't worry. I already promised your father that I would exercise my best behavior."

***

Chapter 38

April felt ill at ease seeing a tall, striking brunette emerge from the car behind her. She looked for any sign of Quinn as the other young woman approached with a welcoming smile.

"Hi, are you April?"

"Uh...yes. How did you know my name?"

Anna stuck out a hand and introduced herself. "Quinn talks about you all the time. So good to finally meet the girl who put a smile back on his face!"

"Oh...okay. You're from California, right?"

"At present, yes, but born in Pittsburgh. Have you and Quinn been dating long?"

"We've only gone out once aside from hanging together at school."

"Sounds like I need to have a talk with little brother while I'm in town."

"I was shocked he wanted me to meet his family so soon," April said, "but understand why he wants to take things slow. Most boys I know aren't as respectful."

"Not to sound judgmental, but none of Quinn's past girlfriends were worthy of his respect." Anna gave her another smile. "Least until now."

"Thanks."

"I hope he warned you how Mom puts every girl he brings home under a figurative microscope."

April swallowed hard. "He mentioned something about her."

"Don't worry." Anna placed a reassuring arm around her shoulder. "Quinn, Troy, and I will make sure her chirping doesn't get out of hand."

Quinn approached them with Noémie in tow. "April! I should've guessed Czech Mate ambushed you since it wouldn't take this long to get the dessert your mom sent."

Anna pecked his cheek. "Hello to you too, little brother." She hugged Noémie. "Hey, little sis!"

Noémie returned the hug. "You're finally here! Where's Jiri?"

"He had to stay in San Diego for work."

"Aw, man! I hoped he'd come with you."

"You're only disappointed because you won't get any presents this time."

Quinn stepped in with introductions. "Now that you met one sister, here's the other. April, meet Pickle. Pickle, April."

The little girl frowned at him. "Noémie, Quinn. My name's *Noémie*."

"Noémie, Pickle, same difference."

She gave Quinn a playful punch. "No it's not!"

"Why would you call her Pickle when she has such a pretty name?" April asked.

"Dad claims she looked like a big pickle when she was born," Quinn replied. "The nickname stuck."

"Still awful." April turned her attention to Noémie. "Quinn says you're a horse riding champion."

Noémie lit up. "Yeah. You want to meet my horse? His name's Blazing Fire."

"Maybe later, Pickle," Quinn said. "We should help Czech Mate get her bags in the house."

Anna popped the car trunk with her key fob. "I have one whole suitcase on wheels and can manage it myself."

"Wouldn't be a gentleman if I didn't offer to help."

"You guys go ahead with April," Anna replied. "I'll be right there."

***

Chapter 39

"You didn't have to bring anything, April," Alex said as she accepted the dessert covered dish. "You're our guest."

"It's my pleasure, Mrs. Talmadge," April replied. "Mom insisted on sending something with me."

"Please, call me Alex. We're glad to have you."

"Can we help with anything?" Quinn asked.

"Oh, no, I have everything under control. Noémie, go find your dad and tell him dinner's ready."

"Smells great, Mom," Anna said. "What masterpiece did Francine create tonight?"

Quinn pulled out a chair for April. "Francine's gone for the weekend but left homemade bread. Mom made spaghetti. Wait until you taste the new sauce!"

"*New* sauce? What happened to the original and canned kinds?"

"Dad bitched about Mom's old one being too spicy."

"Zesty enough to throw me off games back in the day," Troy said as he entered the dining room with Noémie and took a seat.

"Only you would blame a few bad hockey games on spaghetti sauce," Anna laughingly replied.

"Among other things Mom could list," Quinn added, grinning.

"Don't get smart, boy. Ever try playing with unbearable heartburn?"

"Can't say I have. April, this is Dad."

Troy smiled in her direction. "How do you do? I'm Troy."

"Pleasure to meet you, sir," April replied.

He turned to Quinn. "Where have you been hiding this beauty?"

"April and I wanted to know each other better first, Dad," he said.

"Makes sense. Could someone please pass the bread?"

"Save some for everyone else," Alex said as she handed him a basket. "April, you're a junior at St. Rob's?"

"Yes, ma'am," April replied.

"Any plans after you graduate next year? I heard you did well on the SAT test."

Quinn blanched. *Oh shit, here we go. I knew Mom wouldn't resist playing Twenty Questions.*

"Quinn and I have been discussing colleges lately. I'd like to study either business, early childhood development, or nursing."

Her response intrigued Alex. "Quite a combination of interests."

"I'm still deciding between pediatric nursing or someday opening a day care center."

"You must love children."

"Yes, I always enjoy interacting with Dad's patients when I work in his office. I help the front desk staff when they're shorthanded during evening office hours."

"Have you considered becoming a pediatrician?" Anna asked. "You'd have no problem being accepted into a good premed program with your grades and SAT scores."

April shook her head. "One in my family is plenty, plus college will be expensive enough without me burdening my parents with the additional costs of medical school."

"Not to mention people trying to get free medical advice from her at social gatherings," Quinn said.

April merrily laughed. "If I had a dollar for each time that happens to Dad!"

"I can almost imagine," Alex said.

"He handles everything well, though. May I use your bathroom?"

"Sure. There's one down the hall, third door to your right."

"Thank you." April lightly touched Quinn's shoulder. "Be right back."

"Take your time," he replied. "I have nothing else happening tonight."

Quinn gave Alex a hard stare once April was out of earshot. "Okay, Mom, go ahead. I know you've been dying to make bitchy comments."

"Quinn, she's lovely," Alex raved. "You should've dated her a long time ago."

"April didn't attend St. Rob's until this year. Wait...you *like* her?"

"Of course; what's not to like? Pretty, intelligent, articulate, excellent conversationalist, doesn't dress like a prostitute, didn't gush over every little thing in the house, and has solid future plans. You couldn't have chosen better."

"I agree with Mom," Anna said. "April clearly likes you for the right reasons."

Noémie finished her milk. "April's nice. She wants to see Blazing Fire and got mad at Quinn for calling me Pickle."

"Never thought I'd say this, Quinn," Alex said, "but that girl's perfect for you."

Troy leaned back in his chair with a smug look. "What did I tell you earlier, Al?"

"Don't be full of yourself," Alex said.

"Go ahead; say it. 'Troy, you were right'."

"Fine, you were right. Happy?"

"Elated."

April returned as Alex began clearing the table. "Let me help with the dishes, Alex."

"Thank you, honey; they'll need rinsed before going in the dishwasher," Alex replied. "Anna, could you and Noémie get the dessert April brought?"

Anna rose from her chair. "Sure, Mom. Pickle can help me with the dessert plates."

"I'm not Pickle," Noémie protested. "*Noémie.* Get it right."

***

Chapter 40

"Is this ice rink the only place you've taken your dates?" April lightheartedly asked as she watched him shoot pucks Sunday afternoon.

"No," Quinn replied, "but I needed to get in some ice time on my own before Friday's game and thought we could skate together afterward."

"I'm not on a professional level unless falling on my butt a lot counts."

"Which is why we came here today. You can't get better without a little help."

"You are something else, Quinn Talmadge."

"By the way, my family enjoyed having you for dinner last night."

"I liked them too," April replied. "I bet your parents are a lot of fun."

"Mom and Dad have their moments," Quinn said. "They support me playing hockey yet I'm allowed to cut loose once in a while. Many other guys on the team aren't as lucky."

"Noémie's adorable. She wanted me to ride her horse, but I passed. Whoever said Anna was beautiful should consider that an understatement. She's absolutely stunning and so nice, not stuck up like a lot of hot girls."

"My baby sister loves practically everyone. I was shocked how well Czech Mate received you. She's like Mom, always scrutinizing anyone they perceive as 'questionable.' Mom and Dad told me this morning you should visit more often. They want to meet your folks."

"I'm sure something can be arranged on a night my father's not on call at the hospital. I should warn you he may give your parents the third degree on hockey."

"Can't speak for Mom but I'm sure Dad won't mind." Quinn put aside his equipment and held out his hand. "Now it's your turn to do some skating."

"I still say you're inviting trouble."

"You'll be better by end of the day. Trust me."

Taking a deep breath, April swung her legs over the wall, facing Quinn while holding onto cold metal. Quinn's strong arms wrapped around April's torso and she kept a tight hold on him as she jumped from the wall.

"I seem to find you in my arms a lot lately," he said with a knowing smile.

"Yeah...I kind of noticed that."

Quinn lowered April to the floor in a gentle manner. The sweet scent of his cologne and the way he'd held April exhilarated her as she reluctantly stepped from his embrace.

He helped her put on a cardigan. "Here, this will keep you warm."

"Thank you."

"Try a few moves by yourself," Quinn encouraged her.

April's eyes widened. "You can't be serious."

"You did last week. Come on, give it another shot."

Everything went better for April than expected until she missed a step on the ice and landed on her bottom.

Quinn doubled over in hysterical laughter, his giggle-honk titter echoing through the rink.

"Not funny!" she cried as he helped her stand. "This whole thing was *your* idea!"

"I'm sorry! You're...I can't-"

She smacked his arm. "You're lucky I didn't break my neck."

He covered his mouth in an attempt to restrain himself from laughing further, which made April want to hit him a second time.

Quinn soon composed himself. "We need to work more on your coordination."

"No kidding, smart ass."

"Hold on to me and you'll be fine."

They embraced and quietly skated in lazy circles around the rink on which he often practiced alone, oblivious to the world around them.

"I'm such a klutz," she muttered.

"Yet I still love you."

April stared at him in shock. *"What?"*

"Oh," Quinn replied. "I said that aloud."

"Phil's right about one thing; you do move fast on almost everything."

"Getting dirt from my best friend, eh?"

April held back a giggle. "Maybe."

"Seriously, April, I never met anyone like you. You're different from most girls at St. Rob's. You're smart, funny, love hockey, supportive of my aspirations, you don't go use me as an accessory, don't bitch about every little thing, or fawn over me because my parents are famous."

"You're human like everyone else and deserve to be treated that way."

Quinn captured her lips in a soft, meaningful kiss. "You love to cuddle, get along with the guys, and you'd rather hang out watching Netflix than going somewhere fancy. You're independent as I am but we both know we'll sometimes need each other."

"Even if I'm a fat ass klutz?" she asked.

"Hey," Quinn scolded. "No more of that talk. You have a special kind of beauty, much better than some high-maintenance bullshit the media wants to jam down everyone's throats. Kind of nice to be with a girl who actually *eats.*"

April gave him an affectionate poke. "You aren't bad either."

Quinn's eyes twinkled as his hand slipped into hers. April leaned her head on his chest, both remaining still in center of the ice.

"I like us this way," he said in a soft voice. "Want to go someplace else before I take you home?"

She smiled up at him. "I'm up for anything long as it isn't another ice rink."

***

Chapter 41

April and Quinn remained a solid couple throughout remainder of St. Rob's school year. Mutual friends noticed their happiness and Quinn's teammates often mentioned April's positive influence on their captain.

Each of their parents got along well; Alex and Christine immediately found common ground as both mothers and their respective theater experience. Troy delighted in sharing Rebels' behind-the-scenes anecdotes, reliving his playing days, and quoting hockey statistics with Mark.

April was Quinn's date for Anna's winter wedding. He stood as Jiri's best man and Tamar served as Anna's maid of honor. Jax gave away the bride – albeit grudgingly – not convinced Jiri would make an ideal lifetime partner for Anna.

"Quinn's looking good enough to eat tonight," Tamar whispered at the reception.

April gasped at her revelation. *"Tamar!"*

"He's pretty, though. Don't deny he looked at you through those eyelashes and giggled after 'accidentally' touching your butt on the dance floor."

"Of course he did, but out of embarrassment. I'd expect a gentleman like Quinn to react that way."

"Is it true you're going to Yarmouth with his family for the holidays?"

"Yes. Troy and Alex asked my parents too. Dad had no problem accepting the invitation and got another pediatrician to cover patients while he's gone. I hear the Talmadge's Nova Scotia house is beautiful."

"Lucky," Tamar snorted. "I'm probably going to be stuck in Missouri *again*. I love seeing Papa Harry and Nana Mo at Christmas, but if I have to spend another school break seeing Dad fucking around unshaven and wearing ugly flannel shirt in that God awful cabin of his, I'm going to scream!"

April miserably failed restraining giggles at Tamar's disgusted expression.

Tamar quirked an eyebrow. "Is my misery that funny?"

"Oh, no, no, no!" April replied in protest. "I just had this image of your dad with a beard. He makes me think of some lumberjack with a tragic back story who spends a lot of time staring at distant mountains with his flannel flapping in the wind."

"More like spread out in his shitty recliner in front of the TV drinking beer and cussing at the Kansas City Warriors game when not finding more reasons to ground me and Phil. I have no idea how Mom's dealt with his insanity for almost eighteen years."

"Love." April gazed at Anna and Jiri on the dance floor. "Love can make people do unusual things."

***

Chapter 42

Seeing a few photos of herself included in the society page's coverage of Anna and Jiri's nuptials caught April off balance. She scrutinized each picture with a critical eye, but actually looked beautiful in a silver and green maxi dress that caught the emerald of her eyes, her perfect hair worn loose in shimmering waves.

"My little girl in the society pages!" Christine bubbled when she saw the photos. "You're radiant, sweetheart."

"Mom, the article is about *Anna's* wedding. I doubt anyone else noticed me."

"Stop being ridiculous. A couple of nurses at your father's office can't get over how perfect you and Quinn look together. Are you excited about going to Yarmouth?"

"A little. I need to finish packing."

"Don't bother with much. We're only staying a week and Dad doesn't want us taking more luggage than necessary. Did I mention Alex also invited the O'Freels?"

April looked surprised. "Really? Tamar told me they usually spend the holidays in Missouri."

"Yes, but Marty's relatives will be in Ireland this year. His brother's into genealogy and wanted to further explore the family roots, plus his younger sister never visited there."

"I'm surprised Mr. O'Freel isn't going with them."

"His family's planned itinerary would've conflicted with Marty returning in time for the post-holiday Rebels game. Harper somehow managed to talk him into joining the Talmadges and us instead of having another Christmas in Missouri."

"Phil and Tamar will be happy. They can't stand the cabin."

"So I heard," Christine said with a chuckle. "Harper has long grown tired of it, but tolerates going because she loves Marty and enjoys seeing him happy."

"Sounds like me ice skating no matter how much I suck. The way Quinn's face lights up seeing me on skates makes it all worthwhile."

"The Talmadges have a lake behind their Yarmouth house. Maybe you and the other kids could practice skating while we're there."

"Quinn may have other plans."

"Yes, I never thought of that. You and he probably won't get much alone time in Yarmouth."

"Not with Phil, Tamar, and six adults present," April teased. "Perhaps it's for the best; he and Phil will probably spend more time practicing for the Interscholastic All-Star Game taking place after holiday break."

"Oh yes, Troy said something about Quinn being an All Star."

"He was also named team captain. Phil, Carl, and Trevor are All Stars too. I'm going to the game with Tamar and Lesley."

"Your dad and I wouldn't expect less from you. I'm confident that Quinn appreciates the support."

"Hockey's his dream," April said. "I admire how he wants to succeed on his own instead of riding on the family name."

"He certainly inherited Troy's work ethic," Christine replied. "You don't see such a trait in many kids his age."

"Quinn is a great guy, Mom. He's probably one of the nicest I've met, *especially* considering the prevalence of what Lesley and Tamar call – excuse my language – the average fuck boy. He's the definition of chivalrous; kind, considerate, spontaneous, humorous. Did you see what I got him for Christmas?"

"I don't think so, sweetheart."

"First thing I packed. I hope he likes it."

"I'm sure he'll be delighted with anything coming from you."

April hugged Christine. "Oh, Mom, this is going to be one of the best Christmases ever!"

Christine smiled inwardly as she watched April sprint upstairs to her room. She proudly noted how her daughter had grown from a shy, withdrawn, and self-conscious young woman adjusting to a new academic environment to someone more open and talkative, willing to explore new places and things...all thanks to Quinn and his positive influence.

***

Chapter 43

Spending the holidays in Yarmouth was everything April expected and more. She loved skating on the frozen lake, browsing duty-free shops with Tamar, walking hand in hand with Quinn on a boardwalk behind his parents' home, and watching him hone his hockey playing skills with Phil for the upcoming Interscholastic All-Star Game.

April squealed with elation Christmas morning when she opened Quinn's gift – a custom-made, fourteen-karat gold bracelet with minuscule charms: musical notes, camera, book, mock-up honor society key, nurse's cap (to represent one of her career interests), a diamond heart...and ice skates.

"I left room for this year's St. Rob's charm," he said. "They should be available sometime in January."

"Quinn, this is beautiful!"

He took her hand. "Here, let me help you put it on."

"Open your gift first," April replied.

Quinn's face lit up as he studied the collage she'd spent several weeks compiling, each photo depicting stages of his scholastic hockey career.

"How did you..." he began.

"Your sisters made a few contributions," April replied. "The rest I got from some St. Rob's archives."

"I never saw anything this amazing, April." He gave her a quick kiss. "I can't remember the last time someone put actual thought and effort into a gift."

"I'm glad you like it. Noémie picked out the frame."

"This will look great above my bed at home." He pointed to a photo in the lower right corner. "Is this a card from Dad's rookie year with the Rebels?"

"Yeah. Anna said it reminded her of you and made a nice touch."

"I think you should add artist to your career ambitions."

April laughed. "Okay, I know you love the gift, but don't go nuts."

"Want to go skating after brunch?"

"Absolutely!"

"Preferably *without* Phil, Tams, and Pickle."

April smiled. "Well, it's not like we get many chances to be alone."

"You have gotten better on ice skates. Not wobbly as you were for a while."

"I have a great teacher."

"I think building your confidence helped too." Quinn stood and helped April from the floor. "Come on, let's get ready for brunch before everyone else beats us to the table and scarf everything. You'll need a lot of fuel for skating!"

***

Chapter 44

The second half of St. Rob's term was a whirlwind for April. She attended the All-Star hockey game, Spring Fling, the junior class' New York trip, choir state finals, Honor Society banquet, and was Quinn's date for his senior prom.

The boys' hockey team snared their long-elusive championship, upsetting St. Thomasina when Quinn struck an overtime goal with Phil assisting. April captured every moment on her camera, some photos featured in St. Rob's publicity materials.

Part of April hated to see what she viewed the best year of her school life end; Quinn would graduate soon while she had one year remaining. Her old self-doubts crept to the surface imagining him meeting new people in the real world, his and April's relationship a distant memory.

Several colleges and universities expressed interest in Quinn, but the Atlantic Canadian Junior Hockey League's (ACJHL) Newfoundland Newfies drafted him before he made a final decision on which school to attend.

Quinn leaving to play in a Canadian junior league exacerbated April's insecurities. While thrilled the first step of his dream was being realized, she wasn't unaware players attracting scads of girls, few caring if said athletes were married or otherwise attached.

April spent the final weeks of school crying in her room while she stared a picture of her and Quinn from the prom, fondling charms of the bracelet he gave her for Christmas. Her downtrodden mood didn't go unnoticed by her parents, closest friends, and – most important – Quinn.

All made efforts to distract and cheer April as Quinn's departure grew closer. He reassured her their relationship would never change despite the physical distance.

"You helped me make positive changes in my life, April," Quinn added. "You and my family are my biggest supporters. I'll never forget that."

"You'll meet a lot of girls," she sniffled. "How will you handle them?"

"Same way Dad did before he met Mom. Be nice, buy them coffee, and then go home and either read a 600-page novel or watch The History Channel."

His reply made April laugh. "You're such a geek!" She wiped remaining tears. "Not that I'm complaining, by the way."

"Yeah, no one ever mistook me for Mr. Excitement."

"I love you the way you are. Don't change for anyone and I mean *any*one."

Quinn gave her a tender kiss. "I've come too far for that to happen, sweet stuff."

"I'm going to miss you."

"I'll miss you too, but we can chat on Skype. I'll also open a Snapchat or some other account so we can stay in touch."

"But you hate social media and online messaging."

"For you I'll make an exception. Don't want to risk someone stealing my favorite girl."

"Quinn, please say you're not worried about Carl. He's a good friend but too flirty for my taste. As Dad says, why settle for hot dogs when I already have filet mignon?"

"You see Carl as a *hot dog?*" Quinn asked, amused.

"You're missing the point."

He took April's hands in his. "I have another week before heading to Newfoundland. How about us tearing up on the town? No matter how strange, you pick where we go."

"You'd do that for me?"

"I'd swim naked in any of Pittsburgh's filthy rivers if that's what you wanted."

"How about visiting Philadelphia?" April teased him.

"Now you've gone too far, little lady!"

She wrinkled her nose. "I wouldn't wish that on my worst enemy, let alone boyfriend."

"Glad we're on the same page."

"Do you need help packing? I could come by after dinner."

"Thanks for the offer, but Mom has everything under control."

"How does your family feel about the draft?"

"Mom and Pickle bawled for two nights, Grandma's worried about me being alone in Newfoundland, but Dad, Grandpa, and Aunt Louise are over the moon. Dad started his pro career in juniors, so he filled me in on what to expect. Anna and Jiri sent me a hockey stick from his San Diego company, but I'll only keep it for good luck."

"Sounds like almost everyone took things well."

"Better than I expected." Quinn pulled a small gold chain from under his collar. "Aunt Louise had this made. The charm is both my birth year and jersey number."

April inspected the necklace. "Beautiful! Definitely suits you."

"Speaking of jewelry," Quinn replied and dug in his jeans pocket. "Almost forgot I brought something for you."

She looked befuddled. "What? You already got me a bracelet for Christmas and a locket at prom."

"Sure, but this shows how serious I am not forgetting about you." He handed her a small package. "Open it."

April opened the box and gasped at its contents. "Oh Quinn! Is this...?"

"A promise ring," he replied. "To commemorate that we'll always be together, no matter what."

***

Chapter 45

The early months for Quinn in Newfoundland and April's senior year at St. Rob's were initially difficult for both. They stood in touch with long Skype chats and weekend phone calls throughout remainder of the year.

Quinn sent small presents, reminders he was thinking about April. Mark often teased his daughter when yet another Canadian-postmarked package arrived, but he and Christine were delighted to see April reassured; her mood was lifted by Quinn's calls, Skype sessions, and gifts.

He arranged to have flowers sent for April's birthday – white roses. She loved white roses. Quinn also bought more charms for her bracelet, and she treasured each addition.

Quinn's teammates expressed admiration about his devotion to April. Many lamented how he was too focused on his new career to acknowledge the parades of young women that attended games beyond his saying polite hellos, taking a few photos, and giving autographs. He adored April and never considered cheating, no matter how many nights he felt lonely.

"Guess what?" Quinn asked April in one of their weekend phone calls.

"What? You sound excited."

"I've been named one of two alternate captains!"

"Oh, Quinn, I'm so proud of you. What did your parents say?"

"I haven't told them yet; Francine said no one was home when I called. Mom and Dad are busy working with their staff preparing for the Rebels' season opener. Team will raise its latest Princeton Trophy banner before their game against the Presidents."

"You should try getting hold of your parents again."

"They're likely at the arena. I'll call Dad's office later. How's school?"

"Not bad. Tamar and Lesley asked about you. Mr. Legrand wants me to sing the National Anthem at this year's homecoming game."

"Baby, that's awesome! Think you can get someone to make a video for me?"

"Maybe Carl will if I bat my eyelashes at him a few times," April lightheartedly replied. "He's in Visual Arts club this year and plans to film a lot of homecoming stuff."

"Still trying to steal you from me, eh?"

"Yes, no matter how many times I stress it's not happening. He almost got killed for trying to make a video of Tamar using the bathroom at Tiffany's birthday party."

"What the hell was Sundersson thinking?" Quinn asked with a disgusted tone. "I hope his shenanigans didn't get back to Tams' parents."

"Not to my knowledge. There were a lot of kids drinking and I honestly think Tamar is Carl's second crush even if she's in college. I know I shouldn't blame the victim, but she should've closed and locked the bathroom door."

"Beside the point. Has Tams told you how Phil's doing at university?"

"Not lately, but Marty loves bragging about Phil following in his footsteps playing for their beloved Bull Dogs."

"Why am I not surprised?" Quinn asked with a laugh.

"Tamar says he's a bigger pain in the ass now than before Phil left for college."

"We both know she likes to complain about Marty at every opportunity, but between you and me, every girl should have a dad like him."

"I like Marty," April said. "He's sweet and funny. Did I tell you Trevor got a pet skunk?"

"You can't be serious. Who in their right mind would keep something that gross? Isn't he afraid of getting sprayed?"

"Pet skunks have their stink bags removed to prevent spraying, but Lesley says the thing still smells nasty. Her parents won't let Trevor keep it in the house."

"I don't blame them. Jesus."

"Mr. Stinky lives in their garage and Trevor walks him on a leash."

"Now I *know* the concussion dude got during St. Rob's championship game messed with his head."

April sensed Quinn's squeamishness and changed the subject. "Anything else exciting in Newfoundland?"

"Not much outside games and practices. I'm surprised no one mentioned I'll be an uncle soon."

"What?"

"Anna's pregnant and due sometime after New Year's."

"That was quick. What about her job with the Pacific?"

"She's taking leave next month. The assistant skating coach will fill in until Anna returns."

"Do she and Jiri know what they're having?"

"Yeah. Twin boys."

"Oh my God! That's amazing."

"Anna didn't tell her dad yet. She and Jiri agreed to surprise him when the twins are born."

"What about Alex? They're her grandsons too."

"Sworn not to say anything about the twins' sex to Mr. Ivanka, but okay to tell me and Pickle."

"Congratulations in any case, Uncle Quinn."

"Sounds weird, doesn't it? Never thought I'd be an uncle before turning nineteen."

"Bet you never thought of being an ACJHL team's alternate captain at the same age either."

Quinn heartily laughed. "Good point! Anyway, sorry to end our conversation, but a couple of guys from the team invited me to dinner and should be coming soon."

"Don't apologize," April replied. "We can Skype after your game Monday night. I don't have any exams scheduled next week."

"Monday it is then."

"Good night, Quinn. I love you."

"Love you too, sweet stuff. Talk to you Monday night."

***

Chapter 46

If Troy and Alex ever harbored concerns about Quinn relocating to Newfoundland at a young age, their reservations had dissipated by end of his rookie year. Quinn finished his first season with 77 goals and 81 assists over 70 games, named the ACJHL's Rookie of the Year, and received an Honors Trophy as the league's leading point scorer.

Quinn scored a combined 232 regular season and playoff points, the latter leading the Newfies to a Maritimer Cup Championship. He was chosen the team's Player of the Week six weeks in a row, captured ACJHL's Star of the Month award three times, and was named Juniors Personality of the Year.

"All during our boy's rookie year," Troy said proudly. "I didn't accomplish as much playing juniors my first *two* years."

Alex beamed. "You did *something* right, Papa."

"I wasn't sure the boy could handle juniors barely out of high school, but looks like I've once again been proven wrong."

"If Quinn's doing well now, imagine how far he'd go on a professional level."

"*When* he makes it to the pros," Troy corrected her. "I didn't want to jump the gun and say anything, but rumor has it the AHC's already looking at him."

Alex's eyebrows shot up in surprise. "Any specific teams?"

"None definite, but Gary's been pushing me to get Quinn on the Rebels."

She crossed her arms and snorted. "Gary Greenwood should realize three things: one, I also own the team and appreciate being included in discussions, two, Quinn should stay in juniors at least another year, and three, there's a little thing called salary cap. The Rebels aren't an overly wealthy team, Troy; they never were. We don't have the money for big trades and signing players, whether they're major names or rookies."

"Exactly what I told him. We blew a shit load of cash last season sending Park Burton to Toronto in exchange for Harrison Pyle and a third-round draft pick."

"We'd also have to deal with potential rumors of Quinn playing for the Rebels because we own them. Remember some of the awful things said about Riley McCormick? One of the AHC's elite players, yet people carped about him 'being a big name' only because his father owned the Columbus Cyclones. Riley was able to shut up his critics after being traded to Las Vegas, but I can't imagine Quinn getting a similar break."

"I know, Al, but try to see things a little from Gary's view. I wouldn't mind our son playing on home ice and maybe winning a few Princeton Trophies of his own."

"Get back to me after Quinn finishes another year with the Newfies, and tell Gary I'd like to be aware of any future ideas."

"So noted," Troy replied. "Let's move on to a fun topic. Any ideas what to do for Pickle's birthday?"

"How about the Ohio World Horse Exhibition?" Alex suggested. "Noémie's been begging to go and it's only a three-hour drive each way."

"We're not buying a second horse. Blazing Fire eats up enough of our household budget."

"Noémie's not interested in another horse. She needs new riding gear for next season and it would be nice to for her to meet other riders, trainers, and owners outside the show circuit."

"What the hell," Troy said with a grin. "A kid only turns ten once, and how else should we spend our money? Fancy cars, flashy clothes, mega-mansions? Nah, I'd rather indulge the kids – and your coming grandsons – once in a while."

Alex hugged his shoulders. "Have I mentioned what an amazing man you are?"

"Only a thousand times, but I never get tired of hearing it. Tell Pickle she's got her trip."

"She'll be so overjoyed!"

"Hey, you think we could invite April since the show's on a weekend?" Troy asked. "I know Quinn being in Newfoundland has been rough on her even if they've kept in touch."

"Of course; Noémie adores April. Let me first check if it's okay with Mark and Christine."

The blare of Troy's phone ringing sliced into their conversation and he retrieved it from his pocket. "Shit, wonder who has a bug up their ass this time? No one else usually calls my phone at eight o'clock on a weeknight."

"The joys of team ownership," Alex replied.

He glanced at the screen and smiled. "This is a pleasant surprise. Our favorite Newfoundland Newfies alternate captain and Maritimer Cup Champion."

***

Chapter 47

"What's up, Dad?" Quinn asked in a cheerful tone. "I hear you and Mom have been bragging about me being a Maritimer Champion."

"Good news travels fast," Troy replied.

"Let me guess; April told you guys since Canadian junior leagues aren't exactly big in the States."

"She brought it up during a gab fest with your mother. You know how women love to talk. The entire Rebels organization also knows and is proud of you. You've achieved more playing juniors one season than most do in two or three."

"I'm still trying to wrap my head around everything."

"You'll be fine long as success doesn't *go* to your head."

"Not a chance, Dad. You and Mom taught me better."

"What do I owe the honor of this phone call?" Troy asked.

"I was wondering if you, Mom, Pickle, and April would like to come to the celebration parade in St. John's."

"Depends on when. We've already made plans for Pickle's birthday and not sure how April's folks would feel about her traveling to Canada without them."

"The parade's a week from today. Mark said it would be okay long as April was with you guys. I miss her a lot, Dad."

"I know you do, buddy, and she's always welcome to tag along with us."

"Hey, guess who I saw last week?"

"Hmmmm...give me a hint."

"One of your old teammates."

"Can't be Boris because he's been in Russia since retiring, Preacher's busy with his ministry and the Peace Corps, Brian, Griese, Reggie, Baby Finn, and some others seem to have fallen off the earth, so...Pierre? I heard he's back in Canada."

"No, you'll never believe it. Lenny Walton."

"You have to be shitting me. Last your mother and I heard, he finished doing time for coke possession. What's Lenny doing in Canada?"

"He got out like ten years ago and been clean since. He bought a bush league team with money he'd had left from playing with the Rebels and turned it into a top-notch Labrador Bears affiliate."

"Son of a bitch. I assumed he'd end up dead in some red light district after leaving prison."

"Never assume, Dad. Remember you always told me that? He found a nice girl while living in Labrador and got married. They have three kids."

"Hold it...hold it! Are we discussing the same Lenny Walton, the AHC's biggest man whore second only to Claude Caldwell?"

"Exactly the same dude. Got a little fat and losing some hair, but looks great. Team ownership and being a family man suits him well. He says hello, congratulations on the Harrison Pyle deal, and he thinks Marty being married with twins is hilarious."

"I could say the same about Lenny. Wait until your mother hears about this. What made him get his shit together aside from being locked up?"

"Reverend Brady visited him a lot. Lenny stood in North Carolina with him after getting out of prison, spent another month in rehab, and decided on a new start in Canada."

"Good to know Lenny's walking a clean path. How did you run into him in the first place?"

"He and the Bears' general manager attended a Newfies game scouting junior talent. They wanted to sign me but Nathan Ford turned down the offer."

Christ! I need to get hold of Gary tomorrow. "One reason why your mother and I are comfortable having Nathan as your agent. Mom wants you to stay in juniors at least another year before fielding other offers."

"I was thinking the same, Dad. I think Mr. Ford wants to aim for me getting a full-blown AHC contract rather than setting for some Canadian or American affiliate teams."

"He should have little problem finding a few good deals when the time comes." *Your mother and I would rather have you home...*

"I'll make sure you and Mom are first to know. Make sure Pickle checks out the mail in about a week. I had something made for her birthday."

"You're not going to give your old man a hint?"

Quinn laughed. "Why, so you can tell Pickle? No way! I want it to be a surprise. April knows, but I can trust her to stay quiet."

"You're no fun anymore, boy," Troy kidded.

"Neither were you during juniors, least according to Grandma."

"Now you're being a smart ass."

"Yet you still claim me as your son. Let me know about the parade, okay?"

"I'll have Mom call after we rearrange our schedules and talk to April's folks."

***

Chapter 48

April felt exhilarated from seeing Quinn and his teammates during the championship celebration parade. She beamed with pride when Quinn took his turn hoisting the Maritimer Cup, caught up in excitement of the Newfies winning their first championship in almost a decade.

April met several Newfies players following the parade. She felt silly about being nervous; the group of young men were welcoming and friendly toward her.

Quinn drove her to the hotel. "What did you think of my teammates?"

"They were sweet," April replied. "I look forward to knowing everyone better when I'm not as pressed for time."

"The guys liked you too. Some said you're cute. You're staying with my family one more day, right?"

"Yeah. Troy wants to unwind a little before we head back to Pittsburgh. He and Alex have had a busy few weeks with Rebels business and planning Noémie's birthday trip."

"Want to hang out with me, the guys, and their girlfriends tomorrow? Surely you'd like to do something different from stuff involving my parents and little sister."

"You're right. Much as I love all of them, I'd rather spend my last day in Newfoundland with you."

Quinn walked April to the hotel entrance. "I was hoping you'd say that."

"Tomorrow?" she asked with a warm smile.

He gave her a soft kiss. "Tomorrow. I'll give you a call in the morning."

April thought about the wonderful night as she prepared for bed, optimistic the following day would go as well. She sensed that she and Quinn would remain together through good times and bad. He made her happy in ways no one else – except her parents – had done.

She hoped Quinn continued making her feel that way for a long time.

***

Chapter 49

April and Quinn joined his teammates at Woody's Bar B Q in St. Johns. The restaurant/bar was alive with activity, the ideal atmosphere for a group of boisterous hockey players and their girlfriends.

Service was slow, but humongous, mouth-watering orders of fall-off-the-bone St. Louis ribs, chicken, brisket, macaroni and cheese, baked beans, and coleslaw were worth the long waiting period.

"So April, tell us how Quinn managed to trap you," one of his teammates said.

"He and I met not long after I transferred to St. Rob's last year," she replied. "We shared a lot of classes, were in photography club, and even had a couple of things in common outside school."

Quinn cleared his throat. "We made small talk off and on, but didn't really get together until after Homecoming."

April nodded in agreement. "Quinn asked me to a party, but I got appendicitis before we could go. He taught me to ice skate on some of our dates."

He beamed. "Now my girl skates almost like a pro."

Another player gulped his soda. "Surprised you didn't put a hockey stick in her hand, Talmadge."

"Not yet," Quinn said with a twinkle in his eye.

"No way," April replied. "Hockey's more your thing than mine."

"I'm kidding!" Quinn clasped her hand as he addressed the others. "Did I mention April's a great singer? She performed the National Anthem at this year's homecoming game. I missed it for obvious reasons, but a mutual friend sent me video." He pulled out his phone. "Check it out."

April's face felt hot as she tried to snatch the device from him. "Give me that, you goober!"

"Don't be modest," a girl replied. "Quinn's been talking you up since he came to the Newfies."

"Yeah, we'd love to see Talmadge's video," a third teammate added.

The group huddled and stared in awe at April performing *The Star-Spangled Banner.*

She narrowed her eyes at Quinn. "Remind me to murder Carl after I get home."

He grinned. "What? I love showing off the fact I have a beautiful and talented girlfriend."

"Damn!" another girl exclaimed. "If you can sing the hell out of the States' anthem, I'd love to hear your rendition of *O Canada!"*

Her boyfriend gave April an enthusiastic nod. "Shelia speaks for all of us."

Quinn took a large bite of chicken. "Looks like we found my next project."

"Enough about me," April said. "What's next for you guys now you've won a championship?"

"Time off to enjoy ourselves!" the team cried in unison.

"Hey Talmadge," the Newfies captain said. "I heard the American Hockey Conference is expressing interest in you."

Quinn looked surprised. "News to me, dude. Dad would've said something if that was the case. Probably one of a thousand rumors going around in this sport."

"I wouldn't dismiss them so easy; a few AHC franchises already contacted some of our agents. You're a hot talent that would make a great addition to any team. Shit, look how you helped turn around the Newfies this past year."

"I didn't do it alone. You guys made equal contributions."

"Joe has a point, Quinn," April said. "Maybe the rumors are true."

"I barely finished playing one season in juniors, baby. People like to assume stuff because who my parents are. If I'm going to make a leap to the pros, I want it done on my own merit."

"You will," she replied, "but be prepared to grab the brass ring when it presents itself."

***

PART FOUR

Rebel Son

"Forget the stage
Doesn't matter how tall.
I do it all
For the love of the game."

- Timothy Ford, *For Love of the Game*

Chapter 50

Quinn played a total of two seasons with the Newfoundland Newfies before rumors of him among several junior players being pursued by the American Hockey Conference came to light.

Quinn became a hotter prospect after the ACJHL listed him first overall in the AHC Worldwide Scouting Union rankings. Pittsburgh Rebels General Manager Gary Greenwood saw this as one opportunity to turn around the Rebels' previous dismal season, encouraging Troy and Alex to bring Quinn aboard.

"Even if our poor record this season gives us a better shot at first-round picks, there's no guarantee we'll get him, Gary," Troy said. "Five other teams with better salary caps are salivating at the thought of having Quinn play for them."

"Nothing's impossible, Troy. You and Alex know better than anyone that serious changes are needed for this upcoming season."

"Let's see how well we fare in the draft lottery first."

Prospect of recruiting Quinn aside, the Rebels were in process of undergoing other changes with hope of returning to former Princeton Trophy glory, keeping open minds – and within salary cap – finding strong talent to help reach their goal.

Head Coach Dean Barry retired after nearly two decades and Associate Coach Marty O'Freel took the interim role. Marty salvaged what he could of another lackluster season, but not enough to secure a playoff spot.

Greenwood took little time calling Young Rebels coach Ed McCoy when Marty declined becoming head coach on a permanent basis. Marty was content as an associate and eager to resume his previous duties after McCoy's arrival.

Three new players were signed; two Russians with top scoring records in their homeland and a Czech recruited from – interestingly – Jax Ivanka's Prague Capitals.

The Rebels also traded right winger Avery Arlington to Ontario for a fifth-round draft pick and left winger Kip Crompton to San Diego for Phil O'Freel and a third-round selection.

Troy clapped Marty on the back. "Congratulations. Your boy's coming home."

"I have no idea how Gary pulled off that trade nor do I give one hell," Marty replied. "Now all we need is Quinn to complete the transformation into a Princeton-worthy team. Five years missing the playoffs is more than enough."

"As I told Gary, let's see what the draft lottery brings."

"How is Quinn?"

"Doing well considering the amount of AHC teams clamoring to get him, but Nathan has everything under control."

"We have most of St. Rob's last championship team now playing for the Rebels; Connor Williams, Trevor St. Cloud, Jay Gold, and now we're getting Phil. He helped his university win First Division National Championships two years in a row before the Pacific signed him."

Troy winked. "Just like his old man."

"Imagine Quinn and the other boys together again, this time as a second-generation Princeton Trophy team."

"Even if we don't get first crack at Quinn in the lottery, some great new guys are already signed. Nevertheless, we're not going to build a championship-caliber team in one season."

"True; look at the Liberty. They haven't won a Princeton in over fifty years."

Troy burst into laughter. "Hardly one franchise I'd use as an example. The Rebels have played far better in their worst seasons. Look how this year all but tanked, yet you almost got us to the playoffs after Dean retired."

"Emphasis on *almost*. Having a taste of being head coach was okay, but not the headache I'd like to deal with long term."

"Too bad, because you'd made one hell of a coach."

"What's the story on McCoy?" Marty asked. "I know he took the Young Rebels to the Hamilton Trophy finals a few times and has a reputation for being a hard ass yet fair guy."

"Which is the kind of leader we need," Troy replied. "Much as I hate to say it, Dean Barry's best years were behind him. Al, Gary, and I were considering releasing Dean before he announced his retirement. I think Ed will bring back fire we lacked the last five seasons."

"Let's hope all these changes work out, Troy. I'm sure a lot of interested parties are tuning in to tomorrow's draft lottery. Poor Quinn; he's probably a nervous wreck."

"He'll be fine. I've experienced pressures of being a first overall draft pick and am helping him much as possible."

"Thank God I avoided such aggravation by being 62nd overall. Quinn's barely twenty years old and known little else except hockey from the time he put on his first pair of skates."

"Haven't most of us?" Troy asked with a grin.

"Yeah," Marty said. "Now Greenwood needs to find a way to get your son's ass back in Pittsburgh."

***

Chapter 51

The Talmadges and O'Freels attended the ACJHL's annual awards ceremony days before the AHC draft lottery. Everyone beamed with pride as Quinn garnered several honors, including Star of Tomorrow and named Personality of the Year second year in a row.

Troy attempted to discreetly wipe joyful tears during Quinn's speech. Alex watched him out of the corner of her eye, barely concealing her amusement, but said nothing.

Her father's emotional state was not lost on Noémie. "It's okay to cry, Dad," she said in a low voice. "I'm proud of Quinn too."

"I'm *not* crying, Pickle," Troy replied. "I have something in my eye."

"Yeah, big tears. I may be a kid, but you aren't fooling me."

Mother and daughter gave each other knowing looks. "Now honey," Alex said, "'something in his eye' is Dad's way of showing how proud he is of your brother."

Troy gave her a dirty look. "You're not helping, Al."

Harper O'Freel put a reassuring hand on his shoulder. "There's no reason to be ashamed of a few tears."

"I'm not crying!" Troy hissed.

Marty cracked a grin. "The hell you aren't."

"Shut up, Marty. You rant and bitch like a grumpy old man after games once the media's out of sight."

"Only on nights the Rebels played like assholes. Quinn racking up awards is a whole different story. You didn't see me bawling when Phil got the Golden Puck Award and Tamar was named Miss Hockey a couple years ago."

"No, but Mom heard you sniffling a few times," Phil replied.

"Busted," Tamar added.

"Busted for what?" Marty asked. "I had a cold."

"'A cold' my eye," Harper said. "Stop heckling Troy and let him enjoy Quinn's night in peace."

Phil changed the subject. "Why didn't April come?"

"She's in Florida with Mark and Christine," Alex replied. "Christine's aunt and uncle are celebrating their sixty-year wedding anniversary, and April didn't want to miss it. She felt bad about not seeing Quinn get his awards, but he encouraged her to be with family."

Tamar let go a low squeal. "Oh how cute! I love hearing about old people being married a long time."

"Yet you and Phil make gagging noises when I much as hold your mother's hand or kiss her," Marty replied.

"Funny, Dad," Phil said. "Now let's be quiet and listen to the rest of Quinn's speech."

Troy gave him an approving wink. "Good idea, buddy."

***

Chapter 52

Quinn stood in a quiet corner talking softly on his phone following the awards show. "Hey sweet stuff, how's Florida?"

"Beautiful," April replied. "My great-aunt and great-uncle renewed their vows in a nice church and then we all had a picnic on the beach. I still feel awful about missing the awards, though."

"Don't worry about it, baby. We'll go to other things together and Phil made video of my speech. Check your email later."

"Tell him I said thanks. How are you managing the AHC hype?"

"I can't understand why everyone's making a fuss over me when there are other talents coming out of juniors."

"Not the time to be modest, Quinn. I hear the Rebels' GM wants to draft you."

"I know. Mr. Greenwood's been driving Mom and Dad nuts. I'd be content with staying in Canada."

"No way, mister! We all want you home."

"If I had any say, the Rebels could have me if it meant being treated like everyone else. Problem is, no one knows for sure who will get first pick until the draft lottery airs this weekend. I could end up with the Cleveland Clippers, Philadelphia Liberty, or some other shit team."

"God, please let it be anyone but Philly. I wouldn't wish them on the world's worst player," April said.

"I thought the Liberty's one of your favorites," Quinn teased her.

"Ugh, not in this lifetime. They have the nastiest fans. Dad and I watched video of Troy's games one day and we could hear the "Talmadge sucks!" chants every time the Rebels played in Philly. People still go on to this day about how Troy tore people a few new eyeballs when things went wrong."

"People kill me bitching about how much Dad complained. Who cares? The world's best players get perks."

"Exactly, and you'll be the same."

Quinn laughed. "I can be outspoken but never on Dad's level."

"Tell me that in a year. You should be spending what little free time remains with your family and friends."

"Love and miss you, baby."

"I love you too, Quinn. I'll keep my fingers crossed while watching the draft lottery. Good luck."

***

Chapter 53

Several hockey analysts speculated the Rebels could land a top three spot in the draft lottery over the next several weeks, but few predicted what happened once the night arrived.

Troy leaped from his seat in the green room. "Fucking hell! I can't believe it!"

Alex walked in after concluding her phone call. "Now what's your problem?"

"Rebels got the lottery's number one spot and picked Quinn!"

She gasped, thrilled. "Are you kidding me?"

"Not in the least."

"That's incredible! Gary's probably pinching himself."

Troy gave her a proud grin. "Our son's finally coming home."

"The media's going to be all over this," Alex said. "Have you seen Quinn since his interview segment?"

"If you're worried about him getting bombarded, relax. Gary has everything in order."

"His shyness with Canadian reporters while in juniors was charming, but I'm not sure if media covering the AHC will be as forgiving."

"That's why we have PR people, Al. They'll work with Quinn like they do rest of the team."

"Yes, but how many first-round draft lottery picks have we gotten since taking over the franchise? This is a far different situation."

"Quinn already has a clean image, so any additional polishing needed will be gravy. Unlike most teams, the Rebels rarely dealt with media nightmares during its fifty-year existence. If he was a good kid for us, he'll make additional efforts not to put a black mark on the team."

"Perhaps I *am* worrying too much," Alex replied.

"You have every right as his mother to be concerned but let's not get ahead of ourselves. Who knows, Quinn may surprise everyone by making a transition from juniors to AHC."

"Hmmm...you may be on to something. He certainly helped April come out of her shell; maybe he'll do the same for some new teammates."

"Quinn has a calming effect on even the toughest people which will work in his favor. He plays with zeal and determination. I know from personal experience that it isn't easy being the best at something, yet he's taken it all in stride. Quinn's going to be okay, Al; he's worked hard his entire life and hasn't forgotten what matters most in this sport – passion for the game."

***

Chapter 54

Ed McCoy's first order of business as the Rebels' new head coach was appointing Quinn as one of two alternate captains. Everyone from hockey analysts to fans questioned McCoy's choice since the regular season was still weeks away, hence Quinn had yet to make his official AHC debut.

McCoy wasted no time firing back at his critics. "How can Quinn Talmadge gain AHC experience if no one gives him a chance? He's more than proved himself by leading Team Canada to three Junior International championships and two Olympic gold medals. I'm confident that Quinn's more than ready for a leadership role with the Rebels, hence appointing him as an alternate captain."

McCoy's controversial decision wasn't the only thing making waves in the Rebels' organization. Troy held a press conference following the draft lottery and announced his own on-ice return.

Alex was aghast. "Troy, have you lost your mind? You haven't played since before Quinn's birth, and the occasional beer league game doesn't count."

"Al, if your ex-husband could stay in the AHC until age fifty, I can do the same for one season."

"Jax didn't have a twenty-year gap between actively playing. What are you trying to prove?"

"Aside from some old videos, Quinn and Pickle never saw me play. What better time to lace up the skates again?"

"You should've thought that when they were younger. Why do I think there's more to this than the kids?"

"Fine, you got me. Father and son side by side could put asses in seats. We didn't exactly had sellouts the past five regular seasons. We were lucky to fill the glass area's first four rows."

"I hope you know what you're doing."

"Trust me, Al, this is going to be great. I've been training like crazy for the past year and more than ready for a challenge."

"So that's why you disappeared so often without telling me. Did Quinn have any knowledge of your genius idea before you announced it at the press conference?"

"As a matter of fact, I ran it by him, Gary, Ed, and Marty. They were excited, to say the least."

Alex crossed her arms and glared. "Thanks a lot for again not discussing something important with your co-owner and *wife.*"

Troy gave her a sly grin. "If it helps, I didn't say anything to Pickle either."

"I'm not amused. All the world's training and practice won't deter your aging body. You can't just go on the ice and pick up where you left off twenty years earlier."

"Jon Halloran did after a decade and look how well he played."

"Until an arrhythmia nearly killed him. Troy, I'm not thrilled but won't stop you since it's all right with the rest of our staff and Quinn. Promise me your crazy idea is only for one season."

"One and done. I'll let you read the contract if you'd like."

"I'll take your word, but will have you pulled the second something goes wrong."

"Nothing will go wrong, Al. I passed the fitness tests. Did I tell you what happened when Quinn had his done?"

"What, aside from him passing with flying colors?"

Troy heartily laughed. "No one could get over Quinn's eyes. One person commented she never saw anyone with natural violet eyes. Those weren't the only things that drew attention, though. When Quinn took off his shirt, a bunch of women ditched their yoga class to get a peek at him. Here's the funny part – most were old enough to be his grandmother!"

"Oh my God," Alex said. "He must've been more mortified than the time I showed April some of his baby pictures. Quinn came in the door as she looked at the one of him at almost two years old curled up naked on our bed. His face must've turned twenty hues of red!"

"You're cruel," Troy replied jokingly.

"I should warn you Quinn may have his own announcement later."

Troy looked stunned. "Now who's keeping secrets since I didn't get anything from the PR department?"

"Probably because Quinn's announcement's only for family. I'm supposed to call Anna and Jiri when he gets home."

"What could possibly...?" Troy began.

"Take a guess," Alex replied. "It's good as mine."

***

Chapter 55

Quinn gathered April into his arms. "Happy birthday, sweet stuff. I'm finally home!"

April giggled, elated to see him. "My birthday was two weeks ago, you goober. You had roses sent to me."

"Not the same as seeing you in person aside from holidays and occasionally during the off season."

"Dad can't wait for the Rebels' regular season to start," April said. "He's been to a couple preseason games and loves bragging to his colleagues about me dating this year's biggest draft pick."

Quinn raised an eyebrow. "I hope he isn't rubbing it in too much."

"Not really; he and Mom are proud of you as I am."

"Speaking of accomplishments," Quinn said, "you look different lately."

"I got a gym membership and work out a few days a week between classes."

"Why? You weren't *that* big."

"I needed to tone up and be a healthy example if I'm going into nursing, Quinn."

"Please say you're not starving yourself on the down low."

April laughed. "Hard to do when Mom's a great cook and Dad gives stink eyes to anyone who doesn't clean their plate."

"Good for them." Quinn led her to a bench near the river. "I made it to the pros, but that doesn't mean I'd like a typical cookie-cutter girlfriend."

"What do you mean?" April asked, confused.

"Look at most of the other guys' wives and girlfriends. I have yet to see one that isn't at least five foot seven, wears a size two, and has flowing blonde hair. You're different, April, and I want you to embrace standing out from the others."

"I appreciate your sentiment, but what does working on myself – without outside influences, by the way – have to do with other types of women men apparently like?"

"What I'm saying is never feel you have to change for me no matter how successful I am in my career." Quinn smiled and pulled a small box from his jacket pocket. He opened the lid, revealing a simple yet elegant engagement ring. "I prefer having a wife who's comfortable being herself."

She gasped. "Oh my God, Quinn!"

"Does that mean you'll marry me?"

"Yes...*yes!*"

April trembled as Quinn slipped the ring on her finger and kissed her. "You have no idea how many times I played out this moment in my head."

"You're right," she replied. "I don't."

"Now I need to make a couple more stops."

"Haven't you done enough for one day?"

"The media's been all over every little thing I've done since being drafted, and I'd rather have both our parents learn about our engagement straight from us rather than news sources or fan web sites that would likely screw up the facts." Quinn clutched her hand. "Come on; it's getting cold and I want to get a head start on traffic."

April rose from the bench. "Think we could stop for some coffee on the way to Troy and Alex's? I think they should hear our news first."

***

Chapter 56

"You kids are *engaged?*" Troy asked, staring at Quinn and April in disbelief. "That's the big announcement?"

Quinn slid an arm around April's waist. "We are, Dad. You always said not to let go of the right girl once I found her."

"Sure, but aren't you a bit young?"

"For God's sake, Troy, stop being a spoil sport," Alex chided him. "I wasn't much older than he when I married you. We went through this same scenario when Anna and Jiri got engaged."

"Yeah, but -"

"Dad, we're not getting married right away," Quinn said. "April's still in nursing school and I haven't yet played a regular season game. We want to lay some solid ground first."

"Well since you put it that way, I have no additional objections." Troy nodded in April's direction. "Plus she's definitely a keeper."

Alex gave Quinn a tight hug. "Our baby's getting married! I'm so happy for you."

"Mom, let up a little on your grip," he protested. "Breathing's an issue."

"Sorry, got caught up in the moment. We need to start planning your big day."

"We've barely been engaged a couple hours and haven't discussed a date."

"Never too early to start gathering ideas. How did Mark and Christine take the news?"

"They don't know yet," April replied. "We stopped here to tell you guys first."

"Kind of a heads up in case someone from the media catches wind," Quinn added. "We didn't want you and Dad caught off guard. By the way, has either of you called Anna?"

Troy gestured to his phone. "Waiting for her or Jiri to pick up."

"Don't forget to put them on speaker," Alex reminded him.

"Way ahead of you, Al."

Jiri answered with a thick Czech accent. *"Ahoj?"*

"Hello, Jiri!" Troy cheerfully replied. "Your favorite stepfather-in-law here. Is Anna home?"

"Ano...yes. Everything good?"

"Never better. Quinn has some news he'd like to share."

"About team? Anna tell me about draft."

"No, this is more personal."

"Oh, okay. I get her on phone."

Anna came on the line within seconds. "Guys, what's going on? Jiri's suddenly acting like a dog chasing its tail."

"My fault," Troy replied. "I told him Quinn had some personal news to share."

"What has the little goof done this time?"

"Hope you're sitting down, Czech Mate," Quinn said.

"I've rarely done anything else since taking maternity leave, little brother."

"Good, because I asked April to marry me."

Anna couldn't believe her ears. *"What?"*

"I said yes!" April exclaimed.

Anna let out a high-pitched squeal. "This is great news! When did you get engaged? What's your ring like? When's the wedding?"

Quinn cut her off. "Czech Mate, calm down and take a breath before you pop those babies in the recliner or wherever you're sitting."

"I'm excited for you two. April, remind me to email some information about the woman who made my gown. She has lots of designs that would look great on you."

"Quinn and I haven't set a date."

"No time like the present to start making plans, future sister-in-law!"

"I told your brother the same thing," Alex said.

"Mom has experience getting together things like this. I bet your parents are over the moon, April," Anna said.

"Quinn and I wanted you guys to know first," April replied. "We're heading to Mom and Dad's afterward."

"Good idea. Pickle's probably beside herself with joy."

"Wait," Quinn interjected. "I knew someone was missing."

"Noémie's at Tessa's house for a slumber party," Alex replied. "Your dad and I will tell her tomorrow."

"Let's hope nothing leaks before then."

"Stop acting paranoid, Quinn," April gently chided him.

"You know how fast things spread when one person gets wind of something and blabs on social media."

"People with a few ounces of smarts rarely believe anything *not* posted by the Rebels' PR department," Anna replied. "Relax, little brother. Save the energy for your big AHC debut and upcoming wedding. Hopefully the next big news I hear is about me and Jiri becoming auntie and uncle."

"Whoa!" Quinn cried. "Let's not go nuts."

"How are your babies, Anna?" April asked.

"Ugh, sometimes it's like I'm carrying a sack of bowling balls. I swear these boys take turns sitting on my bladder and poor Jiri's afraid to let me out of his sight when he's not working. On a positive note, I can't wait to see Dad's face when they're born. He's flying in from Prague two weeks before my due date."

"Is Frida coming too?"

"God no! I doubt my twenty-six-year-old stepmother relishes the thought of becoming a *babička*."

"The 'grandma' role's better suited for your mother anyway," Troy replied with a laugh.

Quinn shot him a puzzled look. "Not a cool thing to say, Dad."

"He's right," Alex said. "I'm ready to be a grandma. Anna, let me know when your dad's coming for sure so I can arrange my schedule around getting the earliest possible flight to San Diego."

"No problem, Mom."

"Quinn and I keep you posted about wedding plans," April said. "I can use any and all help offered."

A loud bang outside interrupted the conversation and startled everyone.

"What the hell was that?" Alex asked, shaken.

Troy glanced out the front window. "Jesus, Marty!"

He grabbed a coat from the foyer closet. "Another possible PR disaster I need to avert. Can take a boy out of the Missouri country, but apparently not the Missouri country out of the boy. I'll be back later."

***

Chapter 57

"Is everything okay?" Alex asked when Troy returned.

He nodded in disgust. "Marty shot a raccoon digging in his garbage and scared the whole neighborhood almost to death. Cops were called, but they let him off with a warning."

"Thank God. Rebels' season starts Thursday night and last thing we need is outside drama, especially from our associate coach."

"That's what I told Marty. Jesus, I swear the man thinks he's still living in the Missouri backwoods instead of Pittsburgh city limits."

"Couldn't he just set a trap or called Animal Control to get rid of the raccoon?" Quinn asked.

"Animal Control isn't worth two shits. They told Marty to find another way to get rid of the raccoon. Our tax dollars at work."

"He got rid of it all right." Quinn put on his coat. "April and I need to leave after she's done in the bathroom. Mark's on call at the hospital tonight and we want to be at their place before he leaves."

"Drive carefully; traffic's a bitch this time of day."

"Another reason we want to get going soon as possible. Practice still on tomorrow morning?"

Troy gave him a wide smile. "Seven-thirty sharp at the Rebels Ice Complex."

"Going to be great to finally join the team practices."

"Right, as if you hadn't sneaked in a few on your own. Ed told me that he and Naomi saw you at arena the other morning."

"You know me too well, Dad."

"You're my son. Would you expect any less?"

"Never."

April appeared in the kitchen and squeezed Quinn's waist. "Ready to go?"

"Whenever you are, sweet stuff." Quinn turned back to his parents. "Can't wait for the season to start! See you guys in the morning."

***

Chapter 58

Quinn made his official debut in the sold out Pittsburgh Rebels-Philadelphia Liberty season opener. He'd sent family members Newfies game videos while in juniors, but nothing made Alex prouder than seeing her twenty-year-old son skating alongside his father in an AHC game, an "A" emblazoned on Quinn's sweater.

Other familiar faces among teammates besides left defeseman Phil O'Freel helped Quinn's smooth transition; the Rebels also drafted defenseman Trevor St. Cloud and goalie Braxton Bishop, son of late Miami Sun Devils goal tending legend Tyson Bishop. Gary Greenwood was determined to build a championship team, and he somehow managed to pull "legacy" names while remaining within the salary cap.

Quinn scored four goals in his debut, something never before accomplished by a rookie, but his first milestone was overshadowed by a Rebels loss to the Liberty in overtime.

"Guess my four goals didn't do any favors after all, huh?" he asked after reporters cleared the men's locker room. "I can almost imagine how the media and fans are picking apart this loss."

A few teammates stared in disbelief.

"Are you serious?" Braxton asked. "Tonight was only one game; we still have eighty-one remaining. Yeah, the last goal shot whizzed over my head, but no ones hears me bitching."

"Still beating up yourself like in the St. Rob's days," Phil said. "Come on, man; you played like a champion to a sold-out crowd, something that hasn't happened for this team in a long time, at least according to Dad."

"A win would've been better, especially with our families here tonight. April brought her mom, and Chris isn't even a big sports fan."

"Trying to convert your future mother-in-law?" Trevor joked.

Quinn managed a laugh. "I hope so!"

"Wouldn't hurt since her baby girl's marrying a player."

"Did you and April decide on a date?" Phil asked.

"Nothing definite, but we've discussed a few possible ones. All we've accomplished so far is April picking out her dress and us agreeing on where we'll have our honeymoon."

"Glad I don't have those headaches at the present time."

"You should consider finding a woman, bro. I hear Marty's been trying to get your ass out of the house since you returned from college."

"Could've fooled me the way he figuratively tap danced when I got traded from San Diego. They didn't want to let me go at first since Tam-Tam and I were the first twins to play for them, but the Rebels' deal was too sweet for Pacific management to pass up."

Quinn jerked his thumb in Braxton's direction. "GM Greenwood already drafted this guy and Trent Collier was called up from the Young Rebels as his backup. Bringing in Tamar would've put us over salary cap."

"Just as well. Dad would've resumed his helicopter father act and she loves San Diego."

Quinn looked stunned. "Tams doesn't miss Pittsburgh? Could've fooled me judging from the way she and April talk on the phone almost every night."

"Well, I suspect there's another reason she's enjoying the her stint with the Pacific. Paul Colbert."

"*The* Paul Colbert? He played on Team USA at Junior Internationals. His overtime goal won them the bronze medal."

"That's the guy," Phil replied. "Tam-Tam's nuts about him and did a poor job hiding it. I honestly think she crossed her fingers and prayed not to be traded."

"Hate to ask, but what do your parents think?"

"I doubt either has a clue, which may be good considering how Dad's overprotective of Tam-Tam."

"She couldn't pick a better guy," Quinn said. "Paul has an excellent reputation on and off the ice. Mom said the Rebels expressed interest in signing him last season, but the salary cap made it impossible."

"Sucks owning a virtually broke ass team sometimes, huh?"

"Yeah, especially one that hasn't been to a Princeton Trophy playoff in five years. Now the media's got me pegged as some kind of savior. I can't do it alone, guys."

Braxton nodded in agreement. "You're right, man. We all need to band together and be the worthy team GM Greenwood had in mind."

"Princeton Trophy or bust!" the others cried.

***

Chapter 59

The sound of skates carving ice cut through the arena's chilly air as April pounded the glass and yelled enthusiastically. Her throat ached, but she was too invested in the Rebels' game versus the San Diego Pacific to care.

Quinn whizzed by her several times, his concentration fixated on maintaining control of the puck and shooting it past Pacific goal tender Tamar O'Freel.

"Come on, Quinn! You got this!" April shrieked.

"Is he your favorite player?" a male voice asked.

April turned to a couple sitting in the next row, her cheeks flushed. "You could say that."

"Sorry," his girlfriend apologized. "We didn't mean to embarrass you."

"No, no; it's okay. Quinn's my fiance."

The buzzer sounded, signaling end of second period with the Rebels ahead 3-2. Quinn spied April as he and his teammates skated toward the locker room, blew a kiss, and mouthed "I love you."

She blew back a kiss and waved. "Love you too."

"What a cute couple," the woman remarked before she and her boyfriend headed to the concourse. "Congrats on your engagement."

April blushed again and smiled, flattered by the comment. "Thank you."

Lesley bounced down to where April waited for third period to get underway. "What a game! Rebels look great tonight, but probably would have gotten more goals if it wasn't for a certain person in the Pacific's net."

"Tamar's on fire, which was a good thing last period," April replied. "The Rebels are doing a great job of being aggressive. I think the Pacific's entire offense is based on chasing the puck and dumping it in, which has also kept Braxton on his toes. When they actually cycled down low, the Rebels struck back with more aggression and forced the Pacific to make a few costly mistakes."

"Well listen to you sounding like a real analyst!"

April laughed. "Memorizing stats with Dad isn't enough. I have to keep up with everything else since I'm marrying a player."

"Not just *any* player," Lesley said, "but one dubbed as the future of hockey."

"Quinn's handling the pressure well, especially since he's skating with Troy. The Rebels' PR department media trained Quinn within an inch of his life and his responses to questions are so measured. Quinn's engaging and polished now, not like when he first joined the team and hid from reporters after games."

"I noticed. Too bad he takes so much shit for standing up to officials. I swear I'll strangle the next person who makes another 'Tattletale Talmadge' joke!"

"Can't say I blame him," April replied. "Some refs either make the wrong calls or miss things altogether. The funny parts are when he and Troy gang up on the refs to call them out on their shit."

Lesley cracked a grin. "Or when father and son were both sent to the penalty box during first period tonight."

"Hey! That wasn't funny at all!"

"I'm kidding, April. Seriously, why has Quinn racked a bunch of penalties? His penalty minutes will catch up with his point numbers at the rate he's going."

"I know. Coach McCoy and GM Greenwood have talked to him several times, obviously to no avail. We both know how stubborn Quinn can be, and these are among times I wish he wasn't. On the up side, he's had an outstanding rookie year so far."

"To put it mildly," Lesley replied. "Think the Rebels could clinch a playoff spot?"

"It would be great to see Troy and Quinn hoist the Princeton Trophy together, but still too early in the season to make any definite playoff predictions, the Rebels having an amazing November or otherwise."

"We can always hope," Lesley said. "I better get back to my seat before third period starts. Mom and Dad are here to watch Trevor play before they head back to London."

"Tell them I said hi. See you later."

April remained alone during the second intermission's final moments, digesting silence on the ice – except a Zamboni making its ubiquitous rounds – from sounds of puck shots bouncing off boards and hockey sticks.

Rebels team members finally scurried onto the ice with the Pacific following close behind. April caught Tamar's eye for a moment and discreetly waved. Tamar smiled and gave her a quick "nothing personal" one in kind before lowering her helmet and positioned herself in the net.

Music booming throughout the arena stopped when a referee dropped the puck as third period commenced. April's eyes darted around the rink as the puck streaked across ice. She clenched her jaw when the Pacific took possession, rushed to score, and tied the game.

She emitted a shuddering breath. *Damn it, Braxton, pay attention!*

Rebels' defense remained solid despite their opponents dominating most of third period. Quinn managed to block several critical shots, preventing additional goals by the Pacific.

Things continued to look dismal for the Rebels despite that bright moment, and it appeared they would blow a 3-0 lead scored during first period when Trevor St. Cloud received a high-sticking penalty, giving the Pacific a power play.

"For God's sake, Trevor," April muttered. "Last thing we need is another penalty."

Her disgust turned to glee as a bizarre moment unfolded before her and other fans in attendance. Phil caught the puck and zipped down the ice with Pacific defenseman Vince Roache on his heels. Roache clipped Phil before he could score, but Roache lost control of the puck and sent it into the Pacific's own goal net.

Tamar loudly protested as the Rebels' goal horn blew. "What the hell, Roache? You're supposed to put it in the *other* net, asshole!"

April hid a smile. *Tamar's her father's daughter all right.*

"Thanks, Roache!" a man behind her bellowed.

April giggled when she noticed Quinn try to turn his back on several cameras and hide his face with one gloved hand to avoid his laughter being caught on film.

Phil, on the other hand, couldn't care less. He doubled over in hysterical laughter, eventually getting Quinn to join him. Phil was the only person who seems to bothered trying to goad Quinn into being less professional in public, and proficient in doing it.

The woman who spoke to April earlier placed a hand on her shoulder "That may be the best goal Phil O'Freel *didn't* make."

"I know! I've seen some offbeat things at these games, but an opponent shooting a goal into the own net has to be the craziest yet. Not that I'm complaining!"

***

Chapter 60

"Not one of our better games," Quinn said as he and April walked to the parking garage. "We squeaked out a win, and only because of Vince Roache's goal botch."

"Poor Tamar," April replied. "I couldn't see her face because of the mask, but could tell she was pissed. Unfortunately, Lesley and I weren't able to catch her after the game."

"Doesn't surprise me. Visiting teams occasionally come out and sign autographs, but usually pack up and head out of town soon as possible in order to minimize contact with opposing fans."

"I'm sure last thing Tamar and her teammates wanted to do tonight was risk being razzed by the Rebels' fans."

"Hell, if I had a night like they did, I would tear ass out of town too. Bad enough they're likely getting crucified by the media."

"Rebels fans are more brutal this season since you joined and Troy returned to playing."

"Bandwagoners," Quinn replied. "They're usually ones that don't care about hockey, only stick around when 'big names' arrive or the home team is on a winning streak. Rebels had a lot of those over the years, but teams in every sport has them."

"You wouldn't believe some things I heard in the stands tonight," April said. "A few Pacific fans in our section got badgered nonstop. 'What number is Townsend's teeth?,' 'Tamar O'Freel goal tends like a girl,' 'Bailey Herring smells like fish,' a lot of 'Shame of you's!' with Bryan Carson's penalty, and a big favorite: clapping to 'Thank you Roachey!' chants after he sent the puck into the wrong net."

"Can't be worse than 'Talmadge sucks!' over and over." Quinn looked amused. "Dad and I can't figure out which of us allegedly sucks."

His comment made April laugh. "This sport rarely has a dull moment."

Quinn opened his car's passenger door for her. "So how are you getting along with other spouses and significant others?"

"The husbands and boyfriends are a fun bunch," April said. "They either rope me into playing fooseball and air hockey or join them on pizza and beer outings. A couple wanted me to go to a football game on Sunday, but I need to get in additional studying for Monday morning's exam."

"You haven't done anything with the girls?"

April rolled her eyes. "I don't want to sound mean or as if I'm above anyone, but most of the WAGs are kind of...well...juvenile, superficial, and boring. I truly like Naomi McCoy and Harper; maybe because Harper's Phil and Tamar's mom, and both she and Naomi are more down to earth."

"Fitting in with the other girls can be tough, but try to give everyone a chance."

"You can't be serious, Quinn. I've had more intelligent conversations with mannequins. Most of the WAGs do practically nothing but brag about high-end restaurants and exotic places they've been and the designer clothes, handbags, shoes, and expensive jewelry they have. Then they'll turn around and complain how we're required to attend games, you guys going on the road as if you controlled the away schedule, and charity work Rebels management 'forces' everyone to do."

"Everyone's competitive to some degree in this organization, sweet stuff."

"I know, but what's wrong with being part of reaching out to the community? Most of the WAGs – except Naomi and Harper – act behind the scenes like we're at an execution every time there's a benefit. I don't see problems with us doing community service; it's not like most of the other girls have real jobs or attend school, and ones with families have nannies for their kids. I carry a heavy course load, work two afternoons a week at Dad's office, and do required clinical rotations, yet *never* complained about charity events. I actually appreciate occasional breaks from studying, rotations, and work."

"Don't be petty, April. You honestly think the female players' men don't one-up each other?"

"Certainly not on WAG level if they do. If all the girls' boasting and whining aren't enough to make me want to puke, I've endured hearing who has the best bag, hottest body, latest plastic surgery procedures, or whose man's the best player. God, Quinn, it's all I can do not to throat punch those materialistic and shallow bitches!"

"Every team requires spouses and significant others to spend time together. You have to make things work."

April huffed and rolled her eyes a second time.

"I'm not saying you have to like everyone, but problems between people can affect the Rebels as a whole," Quinn said. "My parents have traded players due to their spouses and significant others causing drama."

"Okay, but I'll only tolerate WAGs – *barely* – for you and the team. Hanging with the guys? No problem."

He squeezed her hand. "I knew I could count on you, baby. Where do you want to eat?"

April welcomed the subject change. "We haven't gone to the Strip District in a while."

"Spaghetti Warehouse?"

"You read my mind!"

"Your wish is my command. I haven't eaten there in ages."

"I can't stay out much later," April reminded him. "I have a childhood poison prevention quiz tomorrow morning and then have to work at Dad's office from one to five-thirty."

"No problem. I also need to be up early for off-day media interviews and then practice for Friday's game against the Presidents."

"Last home game before two back-to-back road games," April said.

"Yeah. I hope we don't make any stupid mistakes like the last time."

"What will I do without you for three days?" she teased.

He ruffled her hair. "Hey, you managed the entire time I was in Newfoundland."

"Barely, but I love having you home much as possible. I won't whine about your road schedule like the other girls do since traveling is part of the job."

Quinn pulled his car into Spaghetti Warehouse's parking lot. "Least you're used to my long absences."

"Harper giving me advice on WAG life and you playing juniors in Canada for two years helped."

"She's the best for offering perspectives," Quinn said. "She was almost the same age as you when Marty brought her to Pittsburgh."

"Harper had never been anywhere outside San Diego before she met Marty, so things were tough for her in the beginning too."

"She adjusted and flourished, though. Maybe one day you'll share experiences the way she does now."

"I hope. Being a 'WAG in training' certainly isn't what it's cracked up to be."

***

Chapter 61

"Passing's been bad all season," Quinn said following Friday morning practice. "Trevor, Grusev, and Brooks have completely lost their mojo. Brooks looks like he'd rather be somewhere else, Trevor's missed important goals, and Grusev's acted stupid the last several games."

Captain Joe Crawford agreed. "Grusev accumulated a shit load of penalties the last three games and needs to be benched for at least the next two. Presidents are dirty bastards, and then Cleveland's the first stop on our next leg of road games. Quinn, I don't want to sound harsh since you've brought a lot to the team, but racking up close to 40 penalty minutes so far this season doesn't give you a good look as an alternate captain. You need to keep your temper in check."

"I know, Joe. I had the same conversations with Coach McCoy, GM Greenwood, and my parents."

"Troy doesn't have much room to talk. He's done his share of dropping gloves since coming back on the ice."

Quinn gave him a slight smile. "Some things never change."

"I also hate to say this out loud – especially in Assistant Coach O'Freel's presence – but Phil ridiculously lost the puck several times during our last two games. He seems uncomfortable with Ivanov and Dvorak; it's a shame because I looked forward to seeing their line this year."

"I honestly think Marty would agree. The Rebels are still far from a playoff-caliber team in spite of changes made during the off season. Yeah, we won more games, but there are long stretches where we've been inconsistent. The dump and chase doesn't seem to click or the opposing team has figured out everything."

"Our defense has played so-so too," Joe replied. "Replace either Marshall or Decker with DeMarco. Marshall's made the most mistakes so far this season and he's aging, but I must admit his skills are superior to Decker's on a good night."

"Right," Quinn said. "There's also our goalie situation. If Coach wants to keep playing Braxton more, then he should make it clear instead of pushing the two-goalie system by switching Braxton and Collier back and forth."

"McCoy's present system isn't doing much for Collier's confidence and Braxton needs stability if he's going to remain on point," Joe agreed.

"The main dilemma is what to do with Marshall long term. Mom and Dad sunk a lot of money into bringing him back to Pittsburgh; he's a longtime veteran so sending him to the Young Rebels isn't an option. If DeMarco replaces him and plays better, Marshall will just warm the bench and eat up much-needed salary space."

"Now you know why I'll never aim to be a general manager or team owner after retirement," Joe replied.

"Same here. Too many fucking headaches. I don't know how my parents and GM Greenwood keep their sanity."

"Fishing and golf," Troy said as he entered the locker room. "Lots of fishing and golf when I'm not in the mood to badger your mother."

"Hey Dad," Quinn greeted him. "Joe and I were discussing a few things about the team."

"I caught some of it," Troy replied, "Both of you have some great insights. Smart move not mentioning anything in Marty's presence about Phil losing pucks, though."

"Guess it's safe to presume Marty's not taking Phil's recent mistakes well, eh?"

"To say the least. He's already ripped Phil a few new ones and hearing anything further from us will only get Marty's Irish up more. Ed's coming in a few minutes, so you may want to pass any suggestions to him."

"What do you think of the Marshall issue, Dad?"

"The decision to bring back Pete Marshall was more your mother and Gary's idea than mine," Troy replied. "They presumed Pete had some firepower left for one more Rebels run after three killer seasons with the Orlando Gators. Problem is, he's no Jax Ivanka far as playing longevity's concerned. I agree with Joe that Pete's age is catching up with him; he's slowed down since the first Rebels run. Perhaps it's best to bench him a few games, give Denny DeMarco some playing time, and see what direction our defense heads."

"Can't hurt to suggest it to Coach," Quinn said, "but we may tread on dangerous ground since Marshall's one of Coach and Marty's 'go to' players."

"Let me handle Ed and Marty. You boys need to worry more about annihilating the Presidents."

"Nothing will put a better taste in my mouth than to get revenge for the shit fest they gave us during our last meeting," Quinn said. "I'm beyond ready!"

"Now all you need to do is to keep your ass out of the penalty box," Joe replied with a chuckle.

***

Chapter 62

"Come on Quinn, shoot it!" Ed McCoy shouted. "Now!"

Quinn charged the net and aimed the puck past opposing goalie Jaden Crow's glove. The whistle blew, citing a good goal, before the Presidents' coach issued a no-goal challenge.

He expanded his arms, confused. "What the fuck?"

Joe Crawford hightailed toward a referee, Quinn directly behind him. "What's the problem?" Joe asked.

The referee gave him a curt nod. "Offsides challenge."

"Offsides my ass! I made a good goal, least it looked like one from my angle," Quinn argued.

"Another dick move. They wouldn't pull this shit if anyone else drove in the puck," Joe said. "I didn't see anything offsides either."

The referee's expression didn't change. "Play remains under review."

"How long are we talking?" Joe asked.

"Depends on what's determined from viewing the film."

"This is bullshit," Quinn replied. "I made the fucking goal."

Joe placed a hand on his shoulder. "Let me handle everything. Remember what I said earlier about keeping your temper under control? I know it's good, you know it's good; it's just convincing rest of these assholes."

Quinn's eyes remained ablaze. "Fine, but no one better screw us out of the goal."

"We may be waiting a while longer. Toronto stepped in for a more in-depth review."

"Fucking hell. Goal's getting called back, isn't it?"

"We don't know that. Go chill out for a few."

Disgusted, Quinn joined several other players waiting for word from Toronto's AHC officials.

"What are those stripes doing?" Troy asked. "Planning a party?"

"Toronto's dragging its heels," Quinn said.

Phil furrowed his brow. "Why? The goal's good."

"That's what Joe and I tried to tell the assholes, but they still insist it was offsides."

"Bullshit," Troy snorted. "I've play the game long enough to know what's offsides, and your shot's far from it."

"Taking long enough," Phil said. "We'll all be old enough to retire by the time Toronto makes its decision."

"Coach looks like he's ready to stab somebody," Quinn replied.

Phil spotted Marty on the Rebels' sidelines with a stern expression on his face and arms crossed. "Safe to say Coach isn't alone."

Troy glanced at the ceiling. "Come on; what the hell's taking so long? We must've waited for five minutes."

"I guessed six," Phil replied as the referee skated to center ice to announce an official decision.

"After further review, the puck was not offsides. Good goal!"

"Yes!" Quinn cried as loud cheers spread through the stands. "I knew it!"

"I could've told them in five seconds," Troy said. "Now let's get on with the game."

The Presidents remained hungry – and frustrated – when several attempts to get on the scoreboard failed. Furious, team goon Barron Adams charged Quinn, grabbed his neck, and hurled him backwards into the boards.

The referee blew his whistle to stop play as Quinn lay still on the ice. "Washington, number 88, two minutes for boarding."

Fans expressed displeasure at the call, their boos vibrating off the arena's walls while teammates and trainers rushed to check on Quinn. He rose without assistance, shook off the blow, and was escorted to the locker room.

The Rebels didn't take long to double their lead to 4-0 while Adams remained in the penalty box. Kasper Ivanov scored off Maurice Decker's feed and Pete Marshall blasted the puck into the Presidents' net within sixteen seconds before power play time expired.

Joe smirked when the buzzer signaled end of second period. "That will teach the red fuckers to mess with one of our main men."

***

Chapter 63

Trevor St. Cloud plopped on the bench in front of his locker as second intermission got underway. "Quinn narrowly escaped being paralyzed, and the only word the AHC officials chose to hear is *escaped.* Adams' ass needed ejected!"

"Fucking bush league," Braxton replied. "Pro players can tell where they are on the ice at all times. Adams intentionally hurled back of Quinn's head into the boards and only got a two-minute penalty? Troy was pissed."

"Can't say I blame him. I've seen players suspended multiple games for less offenses."

Phil snorted in contempt. "If the hit wasn't an intent to injure Quinn, then I don't know what else to tell you guys. Adams was totally out of position and made up for it with a damn wrestling move. He could've checked Quinn easily and legally if he'd stayed in position."

"Adams decided to take the asshole route, something similar to a belly-to-back suplex into the turnbuckle except he grabbed Quinn around the neck instead of his waist," Joe replied. "That's how someone's neck gets broken, by pulling them backwards into the boards head first. I heard the back of Quinn's helmet hit the boards and then the ice. Scared the shit out of me, but he got up like nothing happened."

"I don't know how he managed not to get a broken neck, broken back, *and* a concussion. I'm surprised he didn't need to go into the concussion protocol room."

"Tough like his old man," Braxton said.

Troy entered the locker room. "You say that like it's a bad thing, Bishop."

"Not in the least, sir. How's Quinn?"

"He's surprisingly fine and will be here in a couple minutes."

"All I can say is thank God helmets are better structured these days," Phil said.

"AHC had no choice but to change their helmet standards after your dad's injury," Troy replied.

"Yeah, I don't want to think what would've otherwise happened if Quinn's had flown off."

The locker room door opened and Quinn entered with Ed and Marty. "Me neither."

Phil grinned at his teammate and longtime best friend. "How are you feeling, man?"

"A little rattled, but nothing that will affect me third period."

"Whoa, whoa!" Ed McCoy cried. "Let's not go nuts. You should sit out at least part of next period."

"I'm fine, Coach," Quinn insisted. "I can play."

"Listen to Ed," Marty advised him. "You may feel okay, but that doesn't mean the possibility of a hidden injury doesn't exist."

"I didn't need concussion protocol, so whatever may be wrong can't be too serious."

Troy placed a fatherly arm around Quinn's shoulders. "I think this is one time I'll side with the coaches, buddy. Marty speaks from experience and Ed wants to play things safe. You should sit out at least a couple shifts."

"Okay, the first two shifts," Quinn replied. "Happy?"

"Not about us being happy, but for your own safety. Gary and your mother want you to see the team doctor Monday morning before we leave for Cleveland."

"Isn't that a bit dramatic?"

"More like additional reassurance. Trust me, buddy, it's better to be safe than sorry, especially after the hit you took tonight."

***

311

Chapter 64

"What did the doctor say?" April asked after Quinn's Monday appointment.

"I'm good to play in Cleveland tomorrow night," he said. "People worried for nothing."

"I wouldn't go far as say 'for nothing.' The hit you took caused many reasons for concern. You could've been seriously injured or killed."

"Friday night wasn't the first time an opposing player came after me and certainly not the last. People are always trying to injure me for some reason, but – except a broken jaw while in Newfoundland – I manage to emerged almost unscathed."

"I may have some theories," April replied.

Quinn raised an eyebrow. "Really? I'd like to hear them."

"You're good, many other teams know you're good, and that irritates the shit out of them. You're no longer the whiny teenager fans and jealous players accused you of being while in juniors. You stand up for yourself, yet don't rely on bad calls from officials for protection. Competition sees you as a threat, and the only way to eliminate a threat is injuring them."

"The old 'they hate me because they ain't me,' eh?"

"Exactly."

"Dad went through the same thing in his early playing days. I'm surprised Adams didn't go after him last night instead of me."

"You were the easier target. Troy's only back for one season, so taking him out wouldn't have served the Presidents much purpose."

"Now that you mention it, injuring an old man wouldn't be much fun for goons like Adams."

"A lot of hockey boards were lit up the entire weekend," April said. "Most agreed you're tougher than you appear; lesser people wouldn't have literally walked away from similar hits."

"People said *nice* things about me online? I'll be damned," Quinn kidded.

"Don't act smart," April chided him. "You scared the hell out of a lot more people than me and your mom."

"Yeah, I saw you talking to Whitney Crawford after the game. Finally warming up to some of the other girls?"

"She and Joe were concerned about you. Whitney needed to vent, and I was the only one around to listen. The more we talked, the more I liked her. She's from a Washington County small town. Her dad's a retired police detective and mom a surgical nurse. Whitney never had a serious boyfriend before winning a VIP meet and greet contest. Joe was among the players she met, and as they say, the rest is history."

"The girl from modest means who captured a captain's heart. Sounds like you two found common ground."

"Whitney's sweet, Quinn. She acts cool and distant around the other WAGs only because she feels insecure and assumes they think she's not 'team captain wife caliber.' The consensus among them was Joe should've married a stunning model like many AHC guys and annoyed he instead chose a wholesome girl next door who's pretty but not 'hot' and a little naïve to boot."

"I'm sure she has the wrong impression of what the other girls think," Quinn replied.

"Doubt it; Whitney can't stand most of them either. I can imagine the shit they talk about me since I'm not a typical WAG far as looks are concerned, but I've learned to no longer care."

"Good for you, baby. I hope you can get the same logic through to Whit."

"I'll try my best. She must have some attractive qualities for Joe to marry her, right? We're going to lunch tomorrow since I'm off work and not on the clinical rotation schedule."

"Planning to trade dirt on your men, eh?" Quinn joked.

April gave him a sly grin. "Maybe."

"You're evil."

"Seriously, I could use more wedding advice."

"I thought you were working on stuff with Mom, Anna, and your mom."

"I still am, but it won't hurt to get suggestions from other people. Alex has Noémie at home, not to mention dealing with team business, Mom's busy during the peak of theater season, and Anna's babies are due in a couple months. They shouldn't be obligated to spend all their time with me, especially since you and I have yet to agree on a wedding date."

"We'll discuss it after this leg of away games."

April laughed. "You said that last time you went on the road."

"I shouldn't keep you hanging so long. Let's get something in place before Anna delivers her twins so she has enough time to recover." Quinn kissed her cheek. "I need to get home and finish packing shit."

"Call me when you get to Cleveland," April said. "Behave yourself."

"Do I have a choice? Dad's my traveling partner."

***

Chapter 65

"I'm ordering room service," Troy said while lounging in a Cleveland hotel room. "You want anything?"

Quinn stuck his head out the bathroom door. "I'll take whatever you're getting."

"Two orders of boiled liver."

"Funny, Dad. You hate liver in any form."

"Spaghetti sound better?"

"With lots of Parmesan cheese. I'll be out in another five minutes."

"What are you doing, setting up camp in the john? You're taking forever."

"I showered and shampooed. Get some food in me and I'm ready to kick Clipper ass all over the ice!"

"Clippers have a few dirty players, so you'll need to keep out an eye for goons," Troy said. "We don't need a repeat performance of last Friday night."

"I'll be fine, Dad," Quinn assured him. "I dealt with worse in juniors and during Junior Internationals."

"Stay out of the penalty box too."

"Jesus, not this lecture again."

"I mean it, buddy. Your penalty minutes and point numbers are almost the same. Not the best look for a rookie, a legacy one in particular."

"Kind of hard to avoid the sin bin when division enemies are always trying to either beat teammates' asses or mine. Joe gave me tips on dropping the gloves, though."

"That explains a lot. Fighting lessons from a captain with the AHC's highest number of penalty minutes."

Quinn cracked a grin. "Not to mention the best GP average this season."

"I'm well aware, smart ass. Your mother and I own the team, remember?"

"Long as I've been alive, Dad. By the way, Joe's wife and April hit it off the other night."

"Yeah? I thought she usually hangs with the women player's significant others since she hates the other guys' wives and girlfriends."

"Hate's a strong word, but April still holds the WAGs in low regard except Harper, Whitney, and Naomi."

"Whitney's a nice girl if a bit shy. She and April are close in age and come from similar backgrounds."

"Can't be easy being the youngest WAGs," Quinn replied. "They had lunch together yesterday. April's seeking additional wedding advice."

"You two set a date?" Troy asked hopefully.

"No, and I promised April we'd discuss one after this string of road games ends."

"What the hell stopped you from picking one sooner?"

"We don't want to steal thunder from the birth of Anna's twins, for starters. Mom should take time to enjoy her new grandsons before getting caught up in my and April's wedding."

"Hmmm. I thought you were dragging your feet for a moment."

"Never, Dad. *Never.*"

A knock came on the door. "Room service."

Quinn smiled at Troy. "Your turn."

"Hmph, it's always my turn. Make yourself useful and hand me that bottle of Tums, will you?"

"You're eating spaghetti with heartburn?"

"You have a fresh attitude tonight, buddy. Be sure to put it to use during the game."

"I'll aim to make at least six goals," Quinn cracked as they sat down for dinner.

***

Chapter 66

A whistle blew, signaling the official start of second period. Quinn positioned himself against Morgan Doan, his jaw clenched with determination, ready to win the opening face-off.

Troy assumed position a short distance away and moved to take the puck Quinn passed him. Troy was among the glue that held together scoring, and didn't miss a beat whacking the biscuit into the Clippers' net.

Quinn noticed Troy clutch his chest moments after celebrating the goal. "Are you okay?"

"I'm good, buddy. Guess that room service spaghetti didn't agree with me after all."

"You don't look well, Dad. Maybe Coach McCoy should bench you rest of the game."

"I'm not missing shifts over indigestion. I made another goal, didn't I? I'm ready for a hat trick!"

"Promise you'll alert someone if you can't continue. I'm worried, Dad; no game is worth risking your health."

"The antacid will kick in shortly," Troy assured him.

Quinn gave him a skeptical look. "Okay."

Troy went on a breakaway and headed toward Chan Torres with great speed. Troy lost his edge, and crashed into Torres, and both rose from the ice unscathed. Troy soared past Torres and Doan, controlling the puck like he did in the old days, and indeed scored the hat trick he'd promised Quinn earlier.

Quinn remained unconvinced his father was all right. He skated toward the bench on a shift break and caught Coach McCoy's attention. "I think something's wrong with Dad."

McCoy looked puzzled. "What do you mean? He scored three goals so far tonight, giving us a comfortable lead."

"I know, sir, but Dad looks pale and keeps holding his chest."

Marty nodded at McCoy. "I noticed the same thing, Ed, and think we should pull Troy as a precaution."

"One shift," McCoy said. "Then we'll go from there."

"Don't say anything to Mom," Quinn replied. "No use worrying her if Dad's really dealing with some minor thing."

Marty placed a hand on his shoulder. "We can keep everything under wraps until intermission, but your mother's bound to ask questions, especially if Troy raises hell after being taken off a shift."

"Maybe I'm overreacting, but better for him to be pissed than me ignoring any possible problem. Remember when Declan Dayton collapsed on the ice not during a Young Rebels game not long after assuring the ref he was okay? I don't want Dad facing a similar fate."

"We'll keep an eye on him," Coach McCoy said. "You'll take Troy's spot on the next shift."

"Thanks, guys," Quinn replied. "I appreciate the help."

***

Chapter 67

Ed McCoy and Marty O'Freel pulled aside Alex at intermission. "We need to talk," Marty said.

She looked alarmed. "What's wrong? Is Quinn showing symptoms from the hit Friday night?"

"He's fine, but concerned about Troy."

"Troy's played fantastic all night. What's the problem?"

"He looks pale and held his chest off and on, least that's what Quinn told us," McCoy said. "Troy keeps insisting it's a bad case of heartburn."

"Has the team doctor told you anything?"

"Question should be having Troy agree to an exam."

"God, he's stubborn. This could be something serious. Let me talk to Troy; he's getting checked out whether he likes it or not."

"Quinn didn't want us to say anything," Marty said. "He was afraid you'd worry over nothing."

"Or his father could have something serious. Thank you both for letting me know nevertheless."

"Keep us posted," McCoy replied.

***

Troy agreed to be examined by the Rebels' physician at Alex's urging. Dr. Robert Bridger expressed his concerns to her and recommended Troy be taken to the nearest hospital for additional tests.

"I don't want to alarm you, Mrs. Talmadge, but he's displaying symptoms of a heart attack."

"Make any arrangements you think are best," Alex said. "I'll let Quinn and coaching staff know before intermission ends that Troy will be at the hospital."

"I have an ambulance on the way, ma'am."

"Thank you, Doctor. I'll have Ed field all media questions and Marty talk to the other players after the game."

"Do you want someone to go with Mr. Talmadge?"

"Let me know when the ambulance arrives," Alex said. "I'll drive behind it to the hospital and can bring him back to our hotel when he's discharged."

"Yes, ma'am. I told 911 to have the ambulance drive around back to avoid any possible disruptions during remainder of the game."

"Good. Tell everyone I'll contact them soon as I hear official word from the emergency room doctor."

***

Chapter 68

"Whitney called and told me what happened," April said to Quinn on the phone. "Is Troy okay?"

"He's under observation for a couple more days," Quinn replied. "GM Greenwood arrived in Cleveland late last night and Mom's staying there until Dad's cleared to go home."

"What happened? Did anyone tell you?"

"Doctors said Dad had a mild heart attack and lucky he got to the hospital when he did."

"Oh my God. How long will he be benched?"

"Permanently," Quinn said. "I think this threw a scare into him. Mom and GM Greenwood also convinced Dad his playing days are definitely finished."

"Oh God. Did he put up a fight?"

"Surprisingly, no. Dad wasn't happy at first, but has eventually suggested someone be brought from the Young Rebels to fill his spot."

"Sounds like he's taking things well."

"Better than anyone expected. I'll check with Mom for any updates before heading to the airport."

"What time's your flight?" April asked.

"We should board the plane by twelve-thirty. We'll have an off day in Vegas tomorrow and then it's back to business Friday."

"Will Troy be able to conduct Rebels business once he leaves the hospital?"

"I don't see Mom and GM Greenwood allowing him to delve back in right away. Dad usually listens to Mom, so it's likely she'll convince him to relax at least a couple weeks once they're home."

"As he should. Lots of rest will benefit Troy in the long run."

"Says the lovely student nurse," Quinn replied. "Maybe you should switch to cardiac care."

"No thanks; I'll stick to taking care of kids."

"I've been wrapped up in so much bullshit I keep forgetting to ask how you're managing school."

"Tough at times, but getting through okay. Surprisingly, I aced the last exam."

"Why would that be a surprise? You're bright, April; you always breezed through most courses."

"An accelerated nursing school program and St. Rob's curriculum are totally two different things."

"You're still a master. When things get rough, keep thinking how you'll have a nursing license this time next year."

"And maybe a wedding ring," April teased.

"We're still discussing an official date when I come home."

"I can't wait. Anna and Whitney already emailed me dress ideas. Harper said her sister-in-law Anne Marie's a talented wedding cake decorator and can probably get a good price quote for ours. Naomi's oldest son is in a band and she's sending a list of their rates."

"I hope you aren't going bat shit crazy on stuff. We agreed on a small wedding, remember?"

"A small wedding doesn't have to be shoddy, Quinn; I've been checking out a lot of nice ideas that won't cost us a king's ransom."

"Good, you had me worried for a minute."

"You honestly didn't think I had anything elaborate in mind? Come on, Quinn; I don't have a need to impress the world like certain high-maintenance WAGS who put every little thing on social media. I like us planning something small and private. Now if we could agree on an actual date, I can get things officially rolling."

"We will, sweet stuff. Now I need to get moving if I'm going to check in with Mom and Dad before boarding the plane."

"Have a safe flight and beat the Dealers!"

"We'll aim to win one for Dad," Quinn said. "Call you tomorrow."

***

Chapter 69

Following a huge victory in Cleveland, the Rebels skated onto Five Hundred Arena's ice, facing inter-divisional rivals Vegas Dealers in a nationally televised game. Troy's recent health crisis and fatigue concerns from playing back to back games were quickly laid to rest when Phil and Quinn scored early first period goals only 34 seconds apart.

The number of physical altercations elevated during the contest, most attributed to numerous on-ice incidents between teams. The most memorable battle sparked when Dealers forward Max DeVille delivered a hard hit on Phil, knocking him to the ice. Phil slowly stood up, blood flowing from his nose.

Quinn charged towards DeVille with burning desire to defend his teammate and best friend. Gloves flew, and the two players immediately grappled with one another. Quinn got the upper hand among "Talmadge sucks!" chants and continued beating down DeVille until teammates on both sides and referees pulled apart the combatants.

"Vegas, number 23, two minutes for roughing," the referee announced. "Pittsburgh, number 77, five minutes for fighting."

"What the fuck!" Quinn yelled in protest and pointed at DeVille. "He was fighting too!"

"Quinn...Quinn," Joe muttered into his ear. "You dropped your gloves and fought first. Take the penalty without any further aggravation."

Quinn skated to the penalty box. "This is bullshit."

He and DeVille exchanged heated words while Marty angrily confronted the referee. "You mean to tell us it's okay for DeVille to get only two minutes when he *blatantly* knocked over Phil after attempting to jam him into the boards, yet Quinn gets five minutes for defending him? Are you stripes out of your fucking minds?"

"Marty," Ed McCoy interjected. "Calm down. We'll have a power play once the penalty kill expires."

"Sorry for going off, Ed. I'm goddamn sick of everyone coming for Quinn."

"Well the kid can clearly defend himself. We'll be fine."

Marty clenched his teeth. "Fuck these filthy-playing Dealers. Let's get more goals and show them who's the better team."

***

"That's my boy!" Troy cheered as he watched the fight between Quinn and DeVille unfold on television. "That's it, buddy; beat the shit out of him!"

A fearful expression crossed April's face. "Troy, are you crazy? Quinn could get seriously hurt from fighting."

"He's also gotten injured playing," Mark said. "You'll have to learn fights come with the territory if you're going to be a hockey wife, sweetheart."

"God, Dad, not you too."

"What the hell is this bullshit?" Troy yelled at the TV. "Five minutes for Quinn, yet the other guy only gets two for trying to murder Phil? Jesus!"

"Will you take a few deep breaths?" April asked.

"I don't appreciate my boy getting screwed over by some striped bastard that doesn't know his ass from his elbow." Troy turned back to the TV. "Atta boy, Marty; give him hell!"

"I'm serious," April said, her voice thick with concern. "You barely escaped having a major heart attack and don't want to risk another."

"I can rest assured at least two people in this room know CPR should that happen."

"Don't try to be funny. Have you ever thought your stubborn foolishness could end up leaving Quinn and Noémie without a dad?"

"Jesus, girl, you've been hanging with Al too much. You're starting to sound like her."

"See, this is why we shouldn't watch hockey with women in the room," Mark said jokingly.

Christine gave both men a stern look. "Don't make April and me get Alex on the phone, Troy. You promised to behave."

"Only way I could get her to shut up before she left for a meeting," Troy kidded.

April emitted a resigned sigh. "At least Quinn has some common sense."

Mark rose from his chair. "I need a beer. Anyone else want something from the fridge?"

"We're good, Dad."

"I'll have a beer too," Troy said. "I feel adventurous."

April shook her head with pursed lips. "I don't think so. Not with your meds."

"Sorry, Troy," Mark added. "Dr. Mellon's a colleague and friend of mine, and I don't want to go against his orders. No alcoholic beverages with medication."

"Then you can lead by example by going without beer for at least a couple hours," Christine replied.

Mark returned to his chair. "You're right, honey. I'll do that."

Troy let out a frustrated groan. "Who's the genius that thought I needed babysitting?"

April gave him an 'are-you-kidding' stare. "Believe it or not, your son."

"Shit, what he and Al don't know won't hurt them."

"No, but it could hurt *you.*"

Troy turned to Mark with a grin. "Nursing school's made an impact on the little lady."

"Indeed it has," Mark replied. "School's given her confidence. Makes me and her mother proud."

April warmly smiled. "Thank you, Dad. You're my biggest influence. Too bad medical school's financially out of reach or I'd gone for my M.D. instead."

"You'll make a wonderful nurse, sweetheart. Everyone at the office marvels how well you've worked with the kids."

"Next thing we know, she and Quinn will have their own," Christine said.

"Mom!" April cried with a laugh. "We haven't even set a wedding date."

"What on earth is taking so long? You've been engaged for months."

"We're choosing a date after he comes back from Vegas, Mom."

A mischievous gleam appeared in Troy's eyes. "Would you prefer the kids be engaged only a week before they married like Marty and Harper did?"

"Are you serious?" Mark asked.

"Yeah. Long story." Troy cheered at the TV screen. "Will you look at that? My boy scored another goal!"

"Kid's racking up a lot of points in his rookie year."

"Closing in on one hundred. Call me biased, but I think Quinn may be the best thing that's happened to this team in a long time."

***

Chapter 70

"People still can't get over the fighting penalty you took last night," Trevor said while waiting for the team plane to be cleared for takeoff. "The old 'let's find a way to fuck over Talmadge.' Anyone else would've gotten the standard two minutes."

Quinn shrugged. "I've gotten aggravation since playing at St. Rob's, but more pissed about Phil being roughed. Far as I'm concerned, beating DeVille's ass was worth getting a five-minute penalty."

"Dude, I don't think you dropped gloves that fast long as we've known each other."

"Isn't that the truth!" Phil said with a laugh. "I knew shit was going down the minute I saw gloves fly. Thanks for having my back, man."

"A returning favor for all the times you had mine," Quinn replied.

"You know what else chaps my ass?" Trevor asked. "All the fucking double standards. You'd been called a pussy if you did nothing. When Rob Forrester hit you in the neck, it was dismissed as 'tough old school hockey.' You're labeled a goon if you act reckless. Everyone bitches about 'making hockey violent again,' yet you've gotten nothing but bullshit when you stood up for yourself or the team. I hope you punch out more assholes. I can name at least a few who deserve it."

Joe turned in his seat. "I had to laugh at the fans who chanted 'Talmadge sucks.' Sure, it must've sucked for them to see Quinn score three times, including the winning goal. When will some fans learn he's better than most anyone on their sorry ass teams?"

"You mean sneaking in the goal with twenty seconds left in third period?" Phil asked. "Fucking epic!"

Quinn chuckled. "Another day at the office." He gave Joe a high five. "By the way, Cap, thanks for the assist. Never would've made that last-minute shot without you."

"Always a pleasure." Joe teasingly addressed others on the plane. "Now see? This is how to respect your captain."

Guffaws and mock boos filled the cabin.

Joe joined in the laughter. "Fuck you all! Let's see some of you morons do better."

"You ain't shit with that fancy 'C' on your sweater, Crawford!" Braxton jokingly yelled from back of the plane.

"You have one smart mouth for a rookie goalie, Bishop."

"My daddy taught me well."

Quinn gave Braxton a wide smile. "In more ways than one, dude. You racked up a lot of stops last night. What's your secret?"

"Same as yours. Keep an eye on the puck. Doesn't hurt to watch guys headed in your direction either."

"Speaking of goals," Phil said. "When Trevor got pushed into Austin Crampton at our game against Columbus, no goal was called, but when the Dealers made no effort to avoid crashing into Braxton, their goal was good. Who thinks such things?"

Marty looked up from his laptop. "Stripes who have no idea what the hell they're doing. I swear they've had a 'let's see how we can screw the Rebels' agenda far back as before my playing days. Fortunately, the Toronto big cheeses had more brains or we'd risked going into overtime."

"People actually play hockey when dinosaurs roam earth?" Kasper Ivanov quipped.

Marty shot him an amused look among laughter from the others. "Keep it up, kid; someday you'll be my age. You're lucky to be talented or I'd have the Talmadges and Greenwood ship your smart ass back to Moscow."

"Dad killed it as a defenseman back in his day, Kasper," Phil said. "I learned my best moves from him."

Ivanov didn't miss a beat. "Yet you have no girl."

Phil grinned. "Did I mention I'm a late bloomer like Dad? He got married at like one hundred years old."

"Hilarious," Marty replied as he resumed working on his laptop. "I was almost thirty-six."

"Still a fossil," Phil replied good-naturedly.

"Wait until you have kids. I hope all of them are like you...or worse."

Quinn gave Phil and Marty horrified stares. "Damn, you guys are brutal today."

"I think Dad needs laid," Phil quipped.

"Not too old to get put across my lap and your ass beat, boy," Marty replied without looking up.

"You know I'm just messing with you."

"Of course; always good to let off steam after road games."

"When is this plane getting off the ground?" Braxton asked. "Seems like we've been sitting forever."

"Waiting for remaining fog to clear," Quinn said. "I think ground crew's also filling the fuel tank."

"Yeah," Trevor answered. "Not a good idea to run out while 30 thousand feet in the air."

"I can't wait to get home. I promised April we'd set a wedding date."

"Finally taking the plunge, huh?"

"Yeah. I've procrastinated long enough and she's finishing school in a few months."

"She's great, bro," Trevor replied. "You and Joe have nice girls doing something with their lives besides practically mooching off you two."

"I'm lucky to have her," Quinn said as an announcement for takeoff came over the PA. "Our wedding will be among the happiest days of my life."

***

Chapter 71

Quinn dozed during the plane ride home, a mask covering his eyes to block any light. Several teammates seated nearby snickered and mocked his occasional soft snoring.

Braxton held up his phone and laughed. "I should make a Snapchat video and call it *The Unseen Quinn Talmadge.*"

"Sure, and risk getting your ass beat when he sees it," Phil replied. "Quinn hates being put on social media unless it's something team related."

"We're on the team plane. Why not let the fans know the real Quinn instead of the media created one?"

"Joke videos don't count, Bishop," Joe said. "Leave him alone."

"Come on, guys. I know neither of you is above pulling a few pranks."

Joe frowned. "We also know the difference between whether it's okay or not to violate someone's space. Quinn's generally off limits unless he's participating."

"Yeah," Phil added. "We're talking about a guy who'd never considered doing anything that would jeopardize him being hockey's current rising star or sullying the Talmadge brand his parents worked hard to build. Quinn doesn't want anything getting between him, hockey, or April, which means no one taking questionable pictures or videos, even if we view them as harmless jokes."

"In that case," Braxton put away his phone, "making the snoring video isn't such a hot idea."

"Laughing won't hurt," Phil said. "I've listened to this shit every night since he and I became traveling partners."

Joe chuckled. "Always taking one for the team, O'Freel."

"Quinn sawing logs is mild compared to Dad."

"Phil talks in his sleep," Marty shot back. "I'm serious. Anyone who doesn't believe me is welcome to ask his mother or better yet, Quinn. And don't get me started on his gas issues. They sound like several rounds of Irish bar fights."

"Mom always said I'm my father's son," Phil replied with a smirk.

"Your mother can be an occasional smart ass. She's lucky she's cute."

Quinn stirred from his slumber and pulled up the sleep mask. "Now who's being a smart ass?"

"Your traveling partner," Marty said.

"Tell me something I don't already know. We anywhere near Pittsburgh?"

"Not for a while yet. Tearing hurry to see the little lady?"

Quinn yawned. "Something like that."

"Can't say I blame you, kid. I remember feeling the same about seeing Harper after road trips early in our marriage."

"News flash; you and Mom are still like horny teenagers after you come home," Phil replied.

Marty peered over his glasses. "I can guarantee you'll act the same once married."

"I'm going back to sleep," Quinn said and pulled down his mask. "Wake me when we land."

The Rebels' plane disappeared from radar an hour later.

***

Chapter 72

"What do you mean *lost?*" Alex asked on the phone. "Are you sure there wasn't a possible radar error or someone failed to tell us about flight plan changes?"

GM Gary Greenwood tapped on her office door. "Everything okay, Alexandra?"

She hushed him and concluded the phone conversation. "Please let me know if anything changes. I'm sure there's some kind of mistake."

"What's wrong?" Greenwood pressed when Alex hung up the phone.

"The team plane's missing, Gary," she replied, trying to hide her fear. "It was last spotted on radar long after reaching Hopewell Township."

"Oh my God; we need to call 911 *now*. Has anyone contacted Troy?"

"Let me call him," Alex said. "Get hold of 911, but keep this on down low much as possible. I don't want the entire office in a panic, or worse, the media crawling everywhere before we know what actually happened."

"I'll tell the dispatcher to have people search the general area where the plane was last seen before disappearing."

"Good idea. Thank you."

"Stay positive, Alexandra."

"I will. Let me talk to Troy and send Quinn a text."

***

"What? *When?"* Troy asked. "Al, slow down. I know you're upset; I can hear it in your voice. Have you heard anything else?"

"Rescue workers are combing an area in Hopewell Township," Alex said. "Gary's keeping in touch with the airport, but we don't know anything definite."

Troy changed clothes while balancing the phone on his ear. "I'm on my way to the office."

"No, don't bother; you don't need the additional stress. There's nothing more anyone can do and I just sent Quinn a text."

"I'm coming, Al. End of discussion. Both of us should be present if something's wrong. Do you know if there were any problems in Vegas prior to takeoff?"

"There was a thirty-minute delay while fog cleared and ground crew filled the plane's fuel tank. Nothing else out of the ordinary."

"Please tell me no one from the media has gotten wind of this."

"Not far as I know. Gary was discreet as possible with 911, but I don't know how much longer we can keep things under wraps."

"Maybe we should contact the families," Troy said.

"No," Alex countered. "Wait until we learn something definite. No use upsetting anyone beforehand."

"We need to have statements ready in case questions arise."

"The PR department's already working on something."

"Okay, I'm in the car now. I'll see you in about twenty minutes. Keep me posted of any changes."

***

Chapter 73

Gary Greenwood rushed into the office where Alex and Troy waited for official word on the team plane's location. "Rescue squads found it crashed in a Hopewell Township field."

The news increased Alex's anxiety level. "Has anyone-"

"I'm sorry to say some bodies were recovered and a few people currently missing. Plane went down far from the expressway and a nearby shopping center or we'd have a far worse tragedy on our hands."

"Any identification of the dead and missing?" Troy asked.

"I'm getting a regularly updated list. By the way, area's been cordoned off from journalists and television cameras."

"Good. We don't need a media circus on top of everything else."

Alex braced herself for the worst. "Is Quinn...?"

"Not among the bodies recovered," Gary replied, "but no one's yet confirmed who's missing."

Troy attempted to reassure Alex. "There's still a chance he's alive, Al." He turned back to Gary. "Are there survivors?"

Gary nodded. "They're being transported to hospitals."

"Which ones?"

"Those with life-threatening injuries airlifted to Presbyterian and the others taken by ambulances to Sewickley Valley Hospital."

Troy rose from his chair. "Al, you go to Sewickley, and I'll cover Presby. Gary, start contacting family members. Better they hear from you than seeing some convoluted report on the six o'clock news."

Gary picked up a nearby phone. "I'll get started while waiting for more updates."

"Can someone call me when Quinn's been found?" Alex asked.

"I will personally see that you and Troy are first to know, Alexandra."

"Thank you, Gary. Please keep us posted on any additional updates."

***

Chapter 74

April hung up the phone with fear in her voice. "Mom, that was Alex. Quinn's plane crashed in Hopewell Township. Some...some people were killed and a few missing."

Christine gasped. "Oh my God! Is Quinn-"

"He's not currently listed as dead. Alex said survivors are being found and taken to hospitals, so there's hope he's among them or – worse case scenario – still missing."

"God, please let him be alive."

"I should call Whitney while waiting for news on Quinn. She's probably worried sick about Joe."

"That's a good idea. She needs to hear from someone in a similar situation, honey."

"No one's found Joe either," April replied. "Waiting for any type of word will have me and Whitney on edge. I hope talking helps."

"Couldn't hurt to try," Christine said. "How's Troy handling everything? The stress can't be good for him."

"Better than expected, least according to Alex. They're trying to get identities of people found so GM Greenwood can notify families accordingly."

"Did she say what caused the crash?"

"No, but a more thorough investigation will get underway once rescuers finish their work."

"Of all nights for your dad to be on call. The hospital's probably in chaos. I wonder if he knows anything?"

"If he does, Dad won't be at liberty to tell us. The Talmadges issued strict orders for medical examiner and hospital personnel to avoid the media and anyone else not directly involved with recovery and investigative efforts."

"I hope everyone's found soon," Christine replied. "It will be dark in a few hours."

"Yeah." April bit her lip, trying to hold back tears at the thought of Quinn lying somewhere alone and possibly confused. "I better make that call to Whitney."

***

Chapter 75

Common areas of each hospital were filled to capacity with families and friends waiting official word on loved ones with wails and shrieks of grief from those informed of the dead audible beyond entrance doors.

Whitney Crawford, Troy, and April sat scrunched together in a nearby corner, barely holding themselves together. April stared at a nearby television, straining to hear news coverage of the crash, while Troy took phone calls and Whitney bit her nails until they bled.

"Finally some good news, if one can call it that," Troy said. "No one else has been found dead."

"Oh thank God!" April gasped, further hoping Quinn was alive somewhere near the crash site.

"Have you heard anything about Joe?" Whitney anxiously inquired.

"No, honey," Troy replied. "Not yet."

"What if he wandered somewhere and died alone? What if someone made a mistake not identifying him? What if...?"

"Whit," April stopped her. "Worrying won't help things. He's officially not among the dead, so that's a good sign."

Whitney swallowed hard and composed herself. "I should call my parents. I don't want them hearing about Joe on the news."

"Thanks for a reminder of sorts," Troy replied. "I need to touch base again with Al and Gary."

April looked puzzled. "Didn't you just talk to them?"

"Yeah, about forty-five minutes ago. At the rate recovery process is going, one or both may have new information."

"Don't you think someone would've called if that was the case?"

"Things are chaotic, which is why we all agreed to stay in touch." Troy dialed a number. "I'll call Al first; hopefully she's heard something about Quinn and Joe."

April spotted her father enter the room. "Dad!"

Mark rushed over and hugged her. "Hey, sweetheart. I just finished treating a patient when the ER got bombarded with survivors. You okay?"

"I guess. Troy told us no more dead passengers were found, but some remain missing."

"Don't lose hope. One of the nurses told me rescuers continue to locate people. Her husband's an EMT."

"Whitney's going crazy. She hasn't heard from Joe and he's not on any lists."

A woman's voice came over the PA system. *"Dr. Stephens to the ER...Dr. Stephens to the ER STAT."*

"I need to go, sweetheart," Mark said. "They have all doctors available tonight working on crash victims, a rare time our specialties don't matter. Call your mother and let her know I'm likely to be here overnight."

"Yeah, go ahead. More people could be coming." *Please let one of them be Quinn...*

April was in the process of returning to her seat as Christine walked in the front entrance. "Mom, I thought you were staying home."

"I couldn't stand not knowing anything much longer. You and Whitney holding up okay?"

"Can't speak for Whit, but I'm managing. I just talked to Dad for a few minutes before he got paged back to the ER. He said to tell you he's likely staying overnight. All medical staff need to be available."

"I expected such. Your father always had a cool head in crisis." Christine nodded towards Troy on the phone. "Has he learned anything about Quinn?"

"I don't know. Troy's touching base with Alex and GM Greenwood often as possible. You'd have to ask him."

"I hope Quinn's found soon."

"Me too, Mom. The longer we wait for some kind of word, the more I worry."

Troy ended his latest phone call and approached them. "Hey, Chris. Here to give your daughter moral support?"

Christine nodded. "Something like that. Have you heard any more news?"

"Yeah; Al told me Phil's in surgery for a compound leg fracture at Sewickley Valley. Ed's also there with a broken hip and concussion. STAT Medevac's on its way here with Marty. Al called Harper and Naomi, and got in touch with San Diego's general manager to inform Tamar."

"Nothing on Joe?" April asked.

"Al didn't mention him, sorry."

"God, poor Whitney."

"Gary's holding a press conference in an hour. Maybe we'll know more then."

A burly man burst through the front doors seconds later. "Everyone listen up! I heard on my police scanner that St. Cloud, Crawford, and Talmadge were just found by two hunters!"

***

Chapter 76

Troy and Alex sat on each side of Quinn's bed in silence, their eyes fixated on his bruised and pale face. They were grateful Quinn survived the grinding crash, yet concerned how present injuries would affect him long term.

Quinn opened his eyes, immediately spotted his parents but not April.

Alex smiled wanly and stroked his hair. "Hey."

"Mom? Dad?"

"We're here, buddy," Troy replied in a low voice.

"April?"

"Christine took her home," Alex said. "April was here most of the night and needed a break."

"Okay..." Quinn glanced at the IV line in his hand, bandages covering the scrapes on his arms. He swallowed the dryness in his throat. "What happened?"

"The team's plane went down in a field near Aliquippa."

"How?"

Troy hushed him. "No one knows for sure. An NTSB investigation is underway."

"Is...is everyone dead?"

Alex fed him a few ice chips. "No, honey. There are other survivors."

"How many?"

"Eight confirmed so far," Troy answered.

Quinn attempted to sit up, but his lower body defied movement. "I...I can't feel my legs."

"Don't worry," Alex assured him. "The doctors told us paralysis may be temporary."

"Don't sugar coat things, Mom. I won't play again, will I?"

"We don't know for sure," Troy said. "You've only been in the hospital less than twenty-four hours."

Quinn bit his lip. "How many players are dead?"

Troy and Alex exchanged worried glances.

"Tell me the truth," Quinn pressed. "I'll find out anyway."

Troy cleared his throat. "Five players, two equipment guys, and a flight attendant."

"Coach McCoy? Marty?"

"Both alive; Marty's upstairs in ICU and Ed's at Sewickley Valley."

"Tams! She must be worried as hell. Did anyone-"

"I contacted the Pacific's general manager," Alex replied. "He granted Tamar emergency leave. She's due to arrive in Pittsburgh sometime this afternoon to help Harper with Phil and Marty's progress."

"Wait...Phil's alive too?"

Troy nodded. "He's recovering from compound leg fracture surgery at Sewickely."

"Anna also knows what happened," Alex said. "Unfortunately, she and Jiri saw news coverage before we had a chance to call."

"She and the babies are okay, right?"

"Yes, but Anna's doctor advised her against flying. She's staying in San Diego as a precaution."

"What will happen to the rest of our season?"

"We planned to postpone until Commissioner Palmer announced cancellation of all AHC teams' remaining seasons," Troy replied. "Ticket holders for upcoming games can either use them during first half of next season or get refunds."

"Fuck...everyone must hate us."

"On the contrary," Alex said. "Gary said our email server crashed earlier from overflow of messages coming in from other teams and their fans, and phones haven't stopped ringing."

"Gary's holding another press conference this afternoon about the NTSB investigation," Troy added. "He'll also address statuses of everyone on board the plane since all have been accounted for and their next of kin notified."

"Quinn," Alex asked, "do you remember anything?"

"We sat for a long time in Vegas because of the fog and I slept for a while after takeoff. Some of the guys woke me goofing off, but I fell asleep again not long afterward. Next thing I knew, Joe and Trevor were carrying me through some woods before the hunters found us." Quinn choked back tears. "Now I'm fucking paralyzed and will end up a burden."

"You'll never be one to people who love you, honey, and it's too early to tell whether or not your condition's permanent."

"April deserves better than tolerating me this way."

"A lesser woman would leave," Alex said, "but I'll bet April disagrees with you. She loves you too much." She pulled the covers to Quinn's neck. "Now get some rest; Dad and I should head back to the office and help Gary keep everything under control."

***

Chapter 77

Quinn began physical therapy the following week. April stood by his side despite protests that she "deserved more of a man." Both Quinn's recovery progress and STAT MedEvac's on-board staff aiding him en route to the hospital inspired April to switch her nursing studies from pediatric to trauma, now focused on becoming a flight nurse.

"I couldn't live with myself holding you down, baby," Quinn said one afternoon. "You deserve a man who can give you a better life."

April frowned and shook her head. "Quinn, I love you and don't give a damn what someone offers me. I'll earn my own way."

"You...you don't care if I never walk again?"

"No, because that will never change the awesome person you are inside."

"I'm now damaged goods, April."

"No you're not! Alex said the doctors think your paralysis isn't permanent, and even if it is, I still want to marry you."

"You mean...?"

"You won't get rid of me that easy, Quinn Talmadge. All relationships have bumps in the road. We'll have a wedding one way or another."

"But you want kids."

"Modern medicine offers many procedures should we need them."

"Nurses aren't exactly rich, baby. I have to find another way to earn my share."

April smiled at him. "Have you heard of sled hockey? Granted it's not on AHC level, but in the event you have permanent paralysis – and I'm optimistic you won't – you can still earn a paycheck doing what you love."

A thoughtful expression appeared on Quinn's face. "Sled hockey, eh?"

"Yeah. A couple players would like to meet and speak with you. One lost his legs in Afghanistan and the other paralyzed from the waist down after being hit by a drunk driver."

"Wait! You're already checking out stuff?"

"I had a feeling you'd be downtrodden, so I researched other hockey-related careers. You could also be an equipment manager or try coaching, but let's not get too far ahead of ourselves until we know for sure your condition won't change."

"You're an amazing woman, you know that?"

"Does this mean no more talk about me finding someone better?"

Quinn gave her a broad smile. "Thanks for giving me a new glimmer of hope, sweet stuff. Hospitals suck and I could've used some cheering up."

"You did the same for me when I had my appendix removed. Alex also told me you're going to HealthSouth for additional rehab once the doctor clears you for discharge."

"I have a long way to go before that happens, sweet stuff."

"You'll like HealthSouth. Dad went there a few years ago after his motorcycle accident and couldn't say enough nice things about the place."

"I didn't know Mark rode motorcycles."

"He used to all the time since medical school, but hasn't owned one since his accident. In any case, if his accident could sway Dad into enjoying less dangerous hobbies, any potential change in your condition could offer new career opportunities. Don't give up, Quinn; many people are rooting for you and I'm here for the long run."

***

Chapter 78

Quinn stood in the hospital little over a month and then transferred to HealthSouth for additional rehabilitation. His legs remained paralyzed, but April, his family, surviving Rebels teammates, and friends offering strong support helped raise his morale. Their positive influences sparked determination for Quinn to open a new chapter of his life, permanent paralysis or otherwise.

Paralympics sled hockey stars Adam Ridge and Norm Marx befriended Quinn during his stay at HealthSouth; while Norm's legs were amputated and Adam paralyzed below the waist, their desire to play hockey remained intact. Both men were eager to have Quinn join their endeavors, with additional encouragement from physical therapist, TC Johnson, and supervising physician Dr. Jeffrey Maddox.

Quinn quickly adjusted to the special sled, his competitive spirit revived as he shot pucks around the ice rink with other players.

"This is awesome!" he exclaimed, whizzing around the rink shooting pucks with other players. "How did you guys know I was interested in learning about sled hockey?"

"Your fiancee contacted me online," Norm replied. "She said you were unable to use your legs after being hurt in a plane crash. I called Adam and we worked with the PT staff in putting something together as part of your rehabilitation. Losing our legs doesn't mean the end of one's life, Quinn; it's only part of starting a new one."

Quinn beamed. "I should've known April was involved."

"Your folks and general manager said she's played a big part in you getting better."

"You talked to my parents and GM Greenwood too?"

"Yep. The entire Rebels fan base is also pulling for you, brother."

"Their support helps a lot." Quinn examined his stick. "Looks like I could use a re-taping."

"Oh, right," Norm said with a chuckle. "Your mother mentioned you taping your own sticks."

"Kind of a routine thing. Dad also used to tape his own."

"How long have you played in the pros?" Norm asked.

"I spent two years in Canada playing juniors and drafted by the Rebels this season," Quinn replied. "Season got cut short after the crash. I thought I'd never play again until April told me about sled hockey. I read a lot about it in the hospital."

"Glad you kept an open mind. You'd otherwise missed a lot of other opportunities."

"I've also considered joining the Rebels' equipment staff next season or even coaching another team someday."

Norm patted his shoulder and grinned. "TC wasn't kidding when he said you had a good attitude."

"Only way I can get stronger, man. All that pitying myself and moping in the hospital did was make me feel worse."

"Having a pretty fiancee must help some."

"You're not kidding! April's been my rock through the whole ordeal."

"She's a great girl. When are you getting married?"

"We decided on a date in the spring. I want to at least stand at our wedding even if I may not walk again."

"Well, don't go crazy. Rehabilitation works best if you take it one day at at time. You have great upper body strength and mastering sled hockey sooner than anyone expected. You beat Adam's ass in less time than most of us."

Quinn shrugged. "Guess I carried over my experience playing standard ice hockey."

Norm ruffled his hair. "No time to be humble, kid. You'll do great no matter what direction you head after rehab."

TC Johnson walked to the rink's edge. "Quinn giving you a hard time, Norm?" he jokingly asked.

"On the contrary, man. He picked up sled hockey faster than Adam and I combined. You should have more like this guy."

"I heard that! Every morning is a battle getting most my patients to PT, and then there's Quinn; awake, dressed, put in his chair, and raring to go."

"Can't accomplish anything sitting around and looking stupid, TC," Quinn said with a bright smile.

"Patients like you make my job easier." TC helped Quinn into his wheelchair. "Now we need to get your hard-working self upstairs for lunch and a little break before the afternoon session."

"You'll know where to find me." Quinn turned to Norm. "Thanks for the game, man. Hope we can do it again sometime before I go home."

***

Chapter 79

"We heard you made some new friends," Alex said when she, Troy, and April came to visit the following weekend since Quinn wasn't scheduled for physical therapy.

"You mean Adam and Norm from the Paralympics sled hockey team?" he asked. "Mom, those guys are incredible! They make maneuvering the sled look easy, though I can say firsthand it's anything *but.*"

April gave him a quick kiss. "I'm glad to see you happy and finding new ways to enjoy yourself."

"I'm fortunate to be alive, sweet stuff. I would've never looked into sled hockey if you didn't tell me about it in the first place."

"Now aren't you glad you listened to me?"

Quinn squeezed April's hand. "More than you know."

"Your physical therapist also gave glowing reports," Troy said.

"TC is the best," Quinn replied. "You know, I didn't want to be here at first and only agreed to do PT because I'd be stuck here for at least two weeks minimum and was bored shitless. Then TC and the occupational therapy ladies showed me how to live a life of quality even if I never again use my legs. TC and April eventually arranged to have Norm and Adam spend one day a week with me at the new ice skating rink downstairs. Now I can't wait to go to PT! I wish we had it on weekends too."

Troy heartily laughed. "I think your fellow patients beg to differ."

"Yeah, TC says he has a few difficult cases. I guess everyone could use an occasional break."

"Including you, buddy. You've come a long way and deserve a reward for all the hard work you've done so far."

"We have some surprises for you today," Alex said.

"Come on; you guys didn't have to do anything."

"I think you'll enjoy what we have in store, honey." Alex faced April. "Tell them it's now okay to come in."

April nodded and sprinted from the room. Quinn heard her speaking in hushed tones with other people in the hallway and then sounds of several footsteps approach his room.

"Slow your ass down, girl!" a familiar male voice bellowed. "I want to get there alive!"

Quinn stared wide-eyed at his parents. *"Marty's* here?"

"Yes, but he's not alone today," Troy replied.

April returned, accompanied by Phil hobbling on crutches and Tamar pushing Marty in a wheelchair. "Look who I found!"

Quinn's face lit with joy at the sight of his best friends and their father. "Wow, this *is* a surprise!"

"Daddy came Wednesday," Tamar replied. "Phil and I thought he'd curb the Crabby Missouri Papa attitude once he saw another familiar face was here."

"Apparently he's given staff a hard time," Phil added.

"You'd bitch too if someone kept trying to twist you in different directions almost every damn day," Marty snapped. "I thought I was going to pass out yesterday and my legs still hurt. Then some OT hag woke me at six-thirty this morning for a lousy bird bath. I can't even walk to the john alone. Jesus, these people make the ones at Presby look like pikers."

"At least you can still use your legs," Tamar replied and glanced at Quinn. "Some aren't as fortunate."

"You're right, sweetheart; I'm being an insensitive dick. Sorry, guys."

"I felt the same way when I first came here, but you have to give therapy a chance, Marty," Quinn said. "Everything the staff does is for our own good."

"Looks like you've come along well. Did you ever want to murder your PT guy?"

"Maybe in the beginning. Why? Are they too rough? Maybe you could request someone else. TC's done me a world of good."

"You have that torture bearer too? I swear he hates me."

"No one hates you, Dad," Phil assured Marty. "You'd be rotting in your room if that was the case."

"Nah, I had enough of that bullshit at Presby. At least the food here is better. Nurses are hotter too."

Quinn broke out laughing. "Harper better not get wind you said that."

Marty winked. "She would know I'm kidding."

Harper appeared in the doorway at that moment. "God, Marty! I was all over the place looking like a fool until a nurse said I could find you here."

"Our fault," Troy replied. "We wanted Quinn to see someone else from the crash doing okay, and your kids arranged to have Marty come with them to see Quinn."

"Few of us are lucky to be alive," Phil said in a solemn voice.

"How is everyone else who made it?" Quinn asked. "Be honest; I'm tired of people not telling me things."

"Coach McCoy's doing great with his new hip; Pete's still recovering from a neck injury and concussion, the two flight attendants and Kasper are going home next week, I'm in this cast for at least another eight weeks, and Joe and Trevor left the hospital last week. Joe also retired from the active roster."

"I'm not surprised. He's been considering retirement since last season," Alex said. "Joe's thirty-eight and played over ten years for the Rebels, so maybe retiring is best."

"He's exploring options off the ice," Phil replied.

"We could use another trainer," Troy offered. "Have him give us or Gary a call once he's back up to speed."

"I'll pass along the message. He and Whitney have also discussed starting a family."

"That's great!" April exclaimed. "She was worried sick when no one located Joe for a long time after the plane went down."

"Thank God for those hunters," Quinn said. "I don't want to think what the outcome would've otherwise been if they hadn't come along."

"Kind of makes you no longer criticize any kind of hunting?" Phil asked.

"You got it, bro. Shame some of the guys didn't live."

Troy bowed his head. "We lost almost half the team."

"Could someone give me a lift to the men's room?" Marty asked. "Hate to cut in on depressing conversation and sound crude, but nature's calling."

Troy rose from his seat. "Not a problem."

"I'll come too," Tamar offered.

"Take your time, Marty," Harper said. "You're still a bit weak. Let Troy and Tamar help you."

"I don't need anyone else watching me piss. I have plenty of audience members among the staff."

"Old man almost died twice and still stubborn as hell," Phil said after Troy and Tamar left with Marty.

Quinn looked baffled. "What do you mean 'almost twice'?"

"Dad went into cardiac arrest during STAT Medevac's transport to the hospital, and then bled out in surgery. He had a small stroke and required six units of blood."

Harper leaned forward. "The doctors said Marty had a lacerated liver. They also removed his gallbladder, appendix, and spleen."

"Jesus," Quinn said. "Explains some of his grouchiness. Sounds like he went through seven stages of hell."

"Marty always had an stubborn streak," Alex replied.

"Part of his Irish temperament," Harper agreed. "I don't know if it was a result of blood loss, stroke, or he'd taken another hard smack to the head in the crash, but Marty was confused for a long time after regaining consciousness. He didn't understand for a long time why Tamar stood in town. I had to tell him several times San Diego already granted her compassionate leave before the AHC canceled its remaining season."

Phil bit his lip. "Dad's condition was rough on all of us, but thank God stubbornness worked in his favor for once."

"Seeing Marty in ICU was especially hard on Tamar," Harper said. "She hadn't called him 'Daddy' since she was six years old. Much as I hate to say it out loud, I think the plane crash brought them closer."

"You're right, Mom," Phil replied. "What scared us most was Dad trying to get out of bed thinking he needed to be at the arena for a game. The nurses eventually had to put an alarm on his bed."

"Not uncommon to do that for fall risk or confused patients," April assured him. "It's a safety measure."

Quinn smiled proudly and nodded in her direction. "Future trauma nurse."

"I thought you wanted to do pediatrics," Phil said.

"I did, but Quinn's recovery and rehabilitation inspired me to change career direction."

"She's finishing soon," Quinn said. "Hopefully my ass will be out in time for a front row seat at graduation."

April clutched his hand. "My graduation's not the only thing planned. We're getting married in the spring."

"You finally set a date?" Harper asked. "Congratulations!"

"We hired the planner who did Anna's wedding. I figured that would allow me more time to concentrate on school and participate in Quinn's rehab."

"Don't expect a royal event like Czech Mate's," Quinn said. "April and I plan to have a small ceremony for only family and close friends. No media until after the fact. I don't want our wedding turning into a zoo."

"Which is why we're keeping the date under wraps much as possible," April replied.

"I hope I'm among the close friends," Phil said with a grin.

Quinn chuckled. "You better clear your calendar after that cast comes off, dude. I need a best man and you top the list of prospects."

Phil gave him a fist bump. "Consider your offer accepted!"

"Is your aunt still creating special occasion cakes?" April asked.

"Anne Marie? Yeah, her cakes kick ass. She made an awesome one for Mom's birthday. Better than anything from a bakery."

"Great; I'll have the wedding planner give her a call."

"Be warned; you may have to tie down Dad somewhere to keep him away from the cake."

"Now what did – or didn't – I do?" Marty asked as Tamar wheeled him into the room.

"You were gone a while," Phil said. "We were beginning to wonder if you fell in."

"Turns out both my pipes needed cleaned and I did everything in peace for a change. Did we miss anything important?"

"Nothing aside from Quinn asking me to be best man at his wedding."

"Well, that's pretty much a given." Marty looked up at Troy. "Did you tell your son the other news?"

"What other news?" Quinn asked.

"Oh my God!" Alex gasped. "I almost forgot with all the excitement. Anna had her boys last night."

"I'm an uncle?" Quinn asked with glee. "That's great! I can't wait to meet the little guys."

"Not sure if they should be described as 'little.' One was nine pounds and the other slightly over ten. Anna needed a C-section."

"How's everyone doing?"

"Perfect. The boys were named Jiri II and Jakub, but Anna plans to call them Jerry and Jack despite how Jax feels about 'Americanizing' names."

"Jiri's probably excited about being a dad."

"That's an understatement," Troy replied. "Having sons redeemed him in Jax's eyes. They can now be in the same room without anyone hiding all the sharp objects."

"Twins can be challenging," Marty said, smiling at Phil and Tamar. "They can also be blessings."

Tamar hugged him. "Oh, Daddy, we love you too."

A jovial aide appeared in the doorway. "There's our Mr. O'Freel!"

Marty emitted a mock groan. "Shit, Estelle, you found me."

"I always do, honey. Time to go back to your room for dinner. Your tray should be here shortly, Mr. Talmadge."

"Thanks, Estelle." Quinn gripped the wheels of his chair. "I'll be washing up in the bathroom."

Alex, Troy, and April gathered their things and prepared to leave. They soon grew worried by prolonged silence in the bathroom.

April tapped on the door. "Quinn? Is everything okay?"

"Never better," he shouted in an elated tone. "One of my feet just moved!"

***

Chapter 80

"Come on, TC," Quinn urged his physical therapist. "Let me try walking to the PT room today. This chair was fine when I couldn't move my legs, but I no longer have any use for it. Give the thing to someone who needs it more."

"Can't break policy, my man," TC replied. "You may be able to walk, but if something happens because you didn't use the wheelchair, my black ass will be on the line."

Quinn gave him a mock pout. "You're no fun."

"Rules are in place for your safety. We'll have plenty of time to work those legs in the PT room."

"I'm holding you to that, TC."

"Dr. Maddox wrote in his notes you started moving your legs over the weekend. I always miss the good stuff."

"Can you believe it? I'd finally accepted the paralysis long before my left foot moved on Saturday. I could stand with an aide's help yesterday afternoon and tried on my own this morning. Feeling my feet on the floor first time since before the plane crash was weird but now I want to do it more!"

TC let go a boisterous laugh. "You'll have rest of your life, my man. You're going to be one of HealthSouth's success stories. I wish more of my patients were as motivated."

"By the way, I had a chat with one Saturday. I've known him for years; he's the Rebels' associate coach and my best friend's dad."

"Wait a minute, are you talking about Máirtaín O'Freel?"

"We call him Marty, but yeah."

"Kind of funny you mentioned the man. He's usually feisty, but gave neither me nor Carolyn from OT a hard time for a change."

"I kind of stressed that a person gets out of therapy what they put into it, and no one recovers any quicker by complaining or being a general pain in the ass."

"Attitude plays a big part," TC replied. "Look how far you've come in the short time you've been here."

"Hey, I have important things happening soon. Can't get anything done with no strength."

TC pushed Quinn's wheelchair through the PT room's entrance. "Now we'll work on showing off your newest accomplishment."

Marty immediately spotted the pair. "Jesus Christ, Johnson, I was hoping you got lost," he joked in a good-natured manner, "but I may actually tolerate your ass today since you brought Quinn."

"Morning to you too, Marty," Quinn cheerfully greeted him.

"Still your usual shy shelf, Mr. O'Freel," TC joshed. "I admit to being a little worried since you haven't given anyone aggravation for a whole morning."

"Keep sending up the little OT cutie I had for my bird bath this morning and I'll act even nicer. Kind of helps she looks like a younger version of my wife."

"Ahhh...I knew something was up when Carolyn said you behaved."

"So what's the first thing on today's torture agenda?" Marty asked.

TC handed him a cane. "You're going for a walk with me and Quinn, my man."

"News flash; the kid can't walk."

"Breaking news," Quinn slowly rose from his wheelchair with TC's guidance. "As of this past Saturday, I *can* walk."

Marty's eyes widened in surprise. "When the hell did that happen?"

"Around dinner time Saturday. I was taking care of a few things in the bathroom and my left foot moved. Everything went uphill from there."

"Miracles do exist. Way to go, kid!"

"Now let's try out those newly functioning legs," TC said.

"Why not?" Marty asked with a grin. "At least I have some inspiration today."

"You're in a good mood," Quinn said. "Why do I think it's not only because your bath was done by a cute Occupational Therapy girl?"

Marty hobbled on his cane beside Quinn and TC. "I have my old Tam-Tam back and the moodier version of her is dust. Did I mention my baby girl has a boyfriend I actually *like?*"

"Yeah, Phil told me about Paul. She's crazy about him."

"Nice kid from a good family and an excellent hockey player. No wonder Pacific's management often sings his praises. Paul treats Tam-Tam like a princess. I didn't think guys like that existed aside from you."

Quinn sported a huge grin. "Too bad your dream of having me as a son-in-law didn't work out."

Marty returned the smile. "Given latest developments, I'll cope. April's a lucky girl."

"I'm grateful to have her."

"I felt the same when Harper came into my life. Christ, my dating life was a disaster before I met her."

"Somehow I can't picture you as the wild guy Mom and Dad described."

"Age and marriage can change a man, kid."

"Anyway, has Coach McCoy contacted you since he got out of the hospital?" Quinn asked.

"We talk on the phone at least twice a week. Already itching to get back on the ice, huh?"

"You could say that."

"Too bad rest of the season's shot. I wouldn't mind getting back to work myself."

"Not to interfere with your conversation, gentlemen," TC said, "but both of you have a long way to go before resuming any type of work."

"No kidding," Marty replied. "I'm already wiped out. I think my blood counts are still a mess; I've never been this tired long as I can remember."

"We'll take a little break before leg work," TC offered.

"Sounds good," Quinn replied. "Walking again wasn't easy as I thought."

"Stick with me and Mr. O'Freel. We'll have you running marathons in no time."

"Getting skates back on his feet will be good enough for me," Marty said with an encouraging smile.

Quinn looked up at both men from his chair. "I'd prefer to start with standing at the altar waiting for my bride. One day at at a time, eh, guys?"

***

Chapter 81

Quinn left HealthSouth following two months of intense rehabilitation, eager to resume both his personal and professional lives. When he didn't practice shots in his parents' basement, Quinn was often spotted alone at the Rebels' practice complex whacking pucks, skates gliding over ice as if the grievous injuries he'd received in a plane crash never existed.

Anna and Jiri brought their twin sons for a visit the following Easter. Quinn adored Jack and Jerry on sight; they'd inherited Anna's mocha curls and blue eyes yet showed early signs of Jiri's thick build. Quinn enjoyed playing doting uncle the entire week, looking forward to the day Jack and Jerry were old enough for their first pairs of skates.

"These boys will make great third-generation players," he commented to Anna.

She groaned in response. "Not you too. Dad already all but reserved spots for them on the Prague Capitals' future roster."

"First step towards making it in the AHC."

April propped Jerry on her lap. "God, Quinn, they're still babies. They'll grow up fast enough without being pushed into hockey before they talk."

"Dad had me in skates early."

Alex set a pot of coffee and mugs on the table. "Your father and grandfather's ideas, not mine, by the way."

"I figured as much ages ago, Mom."

"Dad pushed me too," Anna replied, "but I have no complaints considering how well my life turned out."

Quinn nodded. "Same here, paralysis scare and all."

"Have you stood in touch with the sled hockey players you met at rehab?" Alex asked.

"Yeah; as matter of fact, I invited Adam and Norm to the wedding." He glanced at April. "I hope that's okay."

"Are you kidding?" she asked. "I would've kicked your butt if you *didn't.*"

Quinn gave her a quick kiss. "Have I said what a wonderful woman you are?"

"Only a million times, but I never grow tired of hearing it."

"Your nursing school graduation this weekend will be epic. Looks like the weather's going to cooperate."

"They'll have tents ready in case it rains anyway," April said.

"Outdoor graduations are awesome. Just think, sweet stuff, you'll be a full-fledged RN by the time our wedding rolls around."

"Let's not go nuts, Quinn. Nursing exams aren't easy."

"You'll have no problem passing with your smarts." He lifted Jack from his highchair. "Someone little man's a messy eater."

"So were you and your sisters at the same age," Alex said. She took the baby from Quinn's arms. "Let *Babička* Alex clean that sweet little face."

"Where is Pickle, by the way?" Quinn asked. "I haven't seen her much since coming home."

"She's had a full plate with school, riding lessons, uniform fittings, and horse shows." Alex balanced a fussy Jack as she wiped his face. "Your dad and I let her to go to St. Rob's spring carnival with Tessa as reward for making the honor roll."

"Noémie needs a final fitting for her junior bridesmaid's gown," April said. "We're all scheduled to have them Saturday afternoon."

Alex scribbled a note on the family calendar. "Thanks for the reminder. I'll tell Noémie when she comes home."

Quinn scrunched his face when an offensive odor permeated the room. "Either I'm losing my mind or someone needs a serious diaper change."

April smiled and lifted Jerry. "This guy."

"Oh, Jerry," Anna said and reached for him, "you pooped your pants on April."

"Don't worry about it," April replied. "I'll change him. Consider it practice for when Quinn and I have kids."

"Not for a while yet," Quinn said. "We should first enjoy one another as a married couple."

"Of course," Anna replied. "Not everyone has kids off the bat like Harper and Marty...or my mother for that matter."

Alex frowned. "Don't get fresh, young lady. Your father was as much at fault."

"How well I know, Mom. At least he and Jiri are getting along better since the boys were born."

April chuckled at the exchange. "Mom and Dad had me quick too." She stood with Jerry still in her arms. "Let me get this little guy out of his smelly diaper."

"How's Marty doing since he came home?" Anna asked as she took Jack from Alex.

"Much better," Alex replied. "He can't wait for next season to get underway. At least Marty can play golf again or he'd probably drive poor Harper crazy being home almost all the time."

Quinn grinned at his mother. "Least he finally canned the crabby old man act."

"While we're discussing Marty," Alex said, "he gave me and your dad a message for you to call Ed Monday morning."

A bemused expression appeared on Quinn's face. "Did he say why?"

"Not to us directly, but Marty and your dad speculated that Ed could have major changes in mind for the upcoming season."

"Huh. Guess I'll know more on Monday."

"You're not in any trouble," Alex said.

"What made you...?" Quinn began.

"Your guilty conscience is legend in this family."

April returned to the kitchen with Jerry. "Here you are, one clean baby butt."

Anna took Jerry from her and placed him in a nearby highchair. "Thanks for changing him."

"My pleasure. You must have your hands full as a mother of twins."

"That's an understatement. Dad and Jiri spoiling them silly doesn't help matters."

"What about your stepmother?"

Anna snorted in contempt. "Frida won't much as sit in the same room as the boys unless Dad tells her."

April raised an eyebrow. "That's kind of strange."

"Well, Frida's a piece of work. She didn't like the idea of Dad and her moving to San Diego so he could visit the boys more often." Anna smirked. "Dad won that argument, though."

"I thought your father didn't like America."

"Not as a whole, but he's willing to make sacrifices for his grandsons."

"Jax also enjoys the perks American money brings," Alex commented. "Nevertheless, he always had a knack for getting his way."

"Czech Mate has the same gift," Quinn said with a laugh.

"Keep it up, little brother, and today will be the last time you see your nephews," Anna kidded.

"No it won't. You and Jiri are in the wedding party."

"True; you got me. Can't leave April without a matron of honor. I hope to be rid of the rest of my baby weight by then."

"You already look great. Even Jiri said you're hotter with a few extra pounds."

"I agree," April said. "That reminds me; I need to call Whitney, Tamar, and Lesley about the fittings on Saturday." She faced Quinn. "Did you tell Phil, Paul, Joe, and Trevor about their suit appointments?"

Quinn nodded. "Already done, baby. Speaking of Tams, did you guys hear the rumors?"

Alex turned to him. "What rumors?"

"Dad didn't tell you? Word has it GM Greenwood is trying to get her as the Rebels' new goalie by trade deadline."

Alex pinched the bridge of her nose. "I swear I'm going to kick both their asses."

"Don't kill anyone yet," Quinn said. "Negotiations with Tams' agent and the Pacific are still in progress. Marty's also busting ass to help get her here."

"I'd appreciate people keeping me on the same page once in a while."

"I still miss Braxton, though. Dude cracked up everyone in the locker room. I feel sorry for his mom; no one should bury their own kid."

"Tina's had a rough few years. First Tyson died of throat cancer two years ago and then Braxton killed in the plane crash. Thank God Bella moved to Pittsburgh for that weekend news anchor position or Tina would be totally lost."

"Loved ones dying is hard to endure," Anna said. "I don't know what I'd do if something happened to anyone in our family."

"Me neither, honey, but unfortunately death's part of life."

Alex's phone rang and she glimpsed at its screen. "Looks like dear old Troy remembered to check in after all." She went into another room and answered his call. "Where are you? Francine will have dinner ready in an hour."

"Al, you aren't going to believe this, but Ed wants to talk to Quinn sometime this evening instead of waiting until Monday."

"Yeah, I meant to thank you and Gary for once again keeping me up to date on team business," she sarcastically replied. "I heard from our son about possibly getting Tamar in the upcoming trade deadline. Jesus, Troy, I'm your business partner, not an office secretary."

"I was going to tell you when I came home," he said.

"What's so urgent about Quinn calling Ed tonight?"

"Don't tell anyone yet, but Ed and Gary want him to succeed Joe as captain next season."

Alex gasped, delighted. "Oh my God! I'm speechless!"

"There are no ways to describe how excited I am, Al. Quinn will be the Rebels' second youngest captain at 21!"

"Well, not everyone can be a 19-year-old captain like you were."

"Who cares at this point? I can't wait to see Quinn's face when he learns the news."

"Why not tell him ourselves? No use bothering Ed during dinner if you and I already know."

"I think hearing the decision from Ed firsthand would have more value," Troy replied. "Besides, Quinn never wanted us interfering in his career."

"All right, but it's going to be hard keeping everything under wraps until Quinn talks to him."

"Sure," Troy said, "but I have a feeling our boy will be looking forward to next season more than he already does."

***

Epilogue

Quinn and April married in a simple but elegant ceremony exactly two weeks after she graduated nursing school. They purchased a three-bedroom home near his parents' residence, the basement remodeled as an ice rink, Quinn kept his skill set sharp between practices at the Rebels' facility and arena.

The much-anticipated Rebels' season against the New Brunswick Maritimers opened to a sold out crowd, with Troy, Alex, and GM Gary Greenwood observing from their suite. The night was bittersweet; no dry eyes could be found when the bell tolled during moments of silence in memory of players and staff who perished in the plane crash.

All survivors – minus retired Joe Crawford – returned to the ice among thunderous cheers as each player was introduced. Quinn arrived last to a standing ovation, the C emblazoned on his sweater. He spotted Joe seated near the glass, motioned to have a spotlight shone on his former captain, and tossed Joe a puck in acknowledgment.

April Stephens-Talmadge performed the Canadian and American national anthems as a spotlight shone on Tamar O'Freel standing in the Rebels' net, her goaltender's helmet design memorializing each late Rebels player. An Irish Gaelic insignia appeared on the back, accompanied by initials M-H-O and a *"Give me some sugar, baby!"* quote, paying homage to her father, Associate Coach Marty O'Freel, who now stood proudly stood beside Head Coach Ed McCoy.

Tamar also sported an extra black armband on her sweater embroidered with Braxton Bishop's initials and the dates of his birth and death.

After a strong start, the Rebels' season hit a slump from early November into late December. Bandwagon fans soon clamored to have the "C" ripped from Quinn's sweater, Phil and Trevor traded, and Ed McCoy fired, but hardcore fans stood by the team through its struggles.

Determined to make an impact as captain, Quinn helped the Rebels rise from last to fifth place in their division by regular season's end, clinching a Princeton Trophy playoff spot for the first time in five years. He scored two goals in his first playoff game, but the Rebels were eventually eliminated by Princeton Trophy runners-up Anchorage Eskimos.

Quinn appeared shirtless in *Men's Fashion Weekly* during the off-season as part of the publication's "52 Hot AHC Stars" special layouts. While his wife, mother, sisters, grandmother, aunt, and mother-in-law loved the feature, Quinn was mortified when they showed it to friends and business associates. Women of all ages drooled over the photos, embarrassing Quinn more, and he was relieved when the publication moved on to the next player.

April gave birth to a healthy baby girl, Alexandra Christine – nicknamed Ali – days after she and Quinn celebrated their first wedding anniversary. Ali's arrival thrilled Troy; he enjoyed playing "second grandpa" to Anna's sons, but Ali was his and Alex's first grandchild together, and he doted on her.

April kept her nursing license current though Quinn's playing and endorsement salaries offered considerable security for his family. She accepted freelance jobs allowing her to spend more time with her daughter and considered the idea of opening her own nursing temp agency once Ali was old enough to attend school.

Noémie performed in her last horse show at age fourteen, directing full-time focus on her longtime ambition of becoming a veterinarian.

The Rebels got another chance at the Princeton Trophy playoffs during Quinn's second year as team captain, earning a finals spot against the San Diego Pacific. When it appeared everything would once again slip through the Rebels' fingers, both Trevor St. Cloud and Quinn scored hat tricks in Game Six, defeating San Diego for a championship that previously appeared out of reach.

Quinn held up the trophy at center ice, dedicating it to his grandfather. Parker Talmadge had been in poor health for several months, and not expected to survive much longer.

Parker died quietly the following morning, leaving behind a legacy of Princeton Trophy champions.

***

End

About The Author

L. Anne Carrington is a sports fiction bestselling author and freelance writer/journalist whose previous work covered topics from fiction to news stories, human interest features, and entertainment reviews. She wrote *The Wrestling Babe* Internet column for seven years, a former music reviewer for *Indie Music Stop,* former book reviewer for Free Press (an imprint of Simon and Schuster), and pens several other works which appears in both print and Web media.

One of her freelance articles, *An Overview of Causes of Hearing Loss and Deafness,* was bought by Internet Broadcasting Systems, a company that co-produced NBCOlympics.com for the 2004 Summer Olympics in Athens and the 2006 Torino Winter Olympics in addition to being the leading provider of Web sites, content and advertising revenue solutions to the largest and most successful media companies.

Her acclaimed work in both fiction and nonfiction include *The Cruiserweight* series, *Billy Kidman: The Shooting Star,* and number one hockey best seller *Power Play.*

She resides in the Greater Pittsburgh area.